# KYUSHO-JITSU:

## The

## Dillman Method

## of

## Pressure Point

## Fighting

# KYUSHO-JITSU:

## The

## Dillman Method

## of

## Pressure Point Fighting

### by

## George A. Dillman

### with Chris Thomas

A Dillman Karate International Book

First published in 1992 by:
George Dillman Karate International
251 Mountain View Rd. (Grill)
Reading, PA 19607
U.S.A.


©1992 George Dillman Karate International
All rights reserved
First edition 1992
Library of Congress Catalog Card Number: 92-90024
ISBN 0-9631996-1-7 PB
ISBN 0-9631996-0-9 CB

Printed in the United States of America

## A NOTE TO THE READER

The ideas, techniques, and beliefs expressed in this book
are the result of years of study and practice.  The knowledge
contained within is a synthesis of training which was obtained from
martial arts experts over a period of three decades.  I realize and
understand that other persons are teaching similar theories,
and I commend their efforts at disseminating this vital information.
At the same time, I urge the reader to scrutinize the credentials
and depth of knowledge of all martial arts instructors before
assimilating those ideas into one's personal self-defense system.
**Please use restraint when practicing all techniques contained
within this book. Practice only under supervision
of a qualified instructor.**

Mike Patton (left) with his senior student Tom Smith, presently 6th degree black belt.

## IN MEMORY

This book is dedicated to the memory of Mike Patton, of Carey, Ohio. Mike was my first long-distance student and drove 10 hours each way once a month to study at my school in Reading, PA. He was one of the most serious, dedicated martial artists I have been privileged to know. It was because of Mike's curiosity that I began my search for the true meaning of karate back in the early seventies. If Mike were with us now, he would be the leading advocate of the Dillman Theory.

— George A. Dillman

## DEDICATION

This work is dedicated to my family— Wendy, Josh, and April who make it all worthwhile.

— Chris Thomas

## P. S.

Thanks go to Ralph Lindquist, of Harrisburg, PA, my friend and fellow student back at Harry Smith's school for keeping me in the martial arts.

— George A. Dillman

## ACKNOWLEDGEMENTS:

We would like to gratefully acknowledge the work and assistance of those who have made this book possible. Thanks go to, Ed Lake, Bill Burch, Lloyd Brown and Kimberly Dillman for posing in the pictures and patiently allowing techniques to be applied against them. Thanks to Tom Countryman, Wendy Countryman, and Kim Dillman for the principle photography.

Thankyou to our art director, Sergio Onaga, for his outstanding work.

Thankyou to the DKI instructors, Ralph Buschbacher, M.D., Rick Clark, Rick Moneymaker and David Ellis, D.C., who have spent many extracurricular hours compiling medical research in addition to that obtained by the authors.

A hearty cheer and thanks to the many DKI instructors who have filled-in for the authors while the book was being developed—especially to Sandra Schlessman, Ron Richards, Bill Hatt, Ralph Jenkins, and Chuck Lentz. Also, we would like to thank our DKI instructors elsewhere for their support and enthusiasm for the system.

We also appreciate the encouragement and helpful advice we received from our friends at Ohara / Rainbow Publications.

Finally, we wish to thank the many karate masters and teachers whose generosity in sharing knowledge over the years has contributed so much to our growth as martial artists.

**George A. Dillman**, a 9th degree black belt in Ryukyu Kempo (Tomari-te), recently touted by *Black Belt* magazine as a "Karate Pioneer" is one of the U.S.A.'s best-known and well established martial arts personalities.

*Official Karate* magazine (Nov.1982) described Dillman as "one of the winningest competitors karate has ever known." Dillman was four-times National Karate Champion (1969-1972) and during this period was consistently ranked among the top ten competitors in the nation by major karate magazines. During his nine-year competitive career, Dillman claimed a total of 327 trophies in fighting, form, breaking, and weapons.

Dillman began serious martial arts training in 1961, with Harry G. Smith. He also went on to study with Daniel K. Pai, James Coffman, Sam Pearson, Robert Trias, and Seiyu Oyata. Dillman has always considered himself a student, never a master of the martial arts. To this end he and his wife and students have traveled throughout the United States to meet with and train with various martial arts experts. Because of this perseverance, Dillman's martial arts talents have earned him widespread U.S. media coverage. He has appeared on 35 national TV shows, including: *Real People, Mike Douqlas, PM Maqazine, Evening Maqazine,* and NBC's *Sports Machine.* Dillman has also been featured five times in Ripley's *Believe It or Not*, and has been the subject of over 300 newspaper and magazine articles. Dillman, a professional boxer for three and one-half years, is the only person known to have trained with both Bruce Lee and Muhammad Ali. In May of 1988, Dillman was inducted into the Berks County Chapter of the Pennsylvania Sports Hall of Fame. He was the first martial artist to be included.

More recently, however, Dillman has been traveling the world teaching seminars on pressure points and tuite (grappling) hidden within the old forms. It is this research and scientific dissection of the old forms that is earning him his most notoriety. Never one to shy away from controversy, Dillman has opened-up a formerly secret level of meaning for kata movements and made that interpretation understandable to all.

Dillman continues to be the head instructor for the Dillman Karate International, an organization of 70 schools worldwide, with an enrollment of nearly 7,000 students. Dillman has studied under five 10th degree black belts from Okinawa and is currently furthering his personal study through research, practice, and the sharing of techniques with Professor Wally Jay, Small Circle Jujitsu and Professor Remy Presas, Modern Amis.

**Chris Thomas,** martial artist and writer, began studying karate in 1970, at the age of 12. He holds black belts in three separate systems of karate. Thomas holds the rank of nidan in JKA-Shotokan (awarded by the late JKA master, Masatoshi Nakayama), instructor's grade in Isshinryu karate-do, and a master's grade in Ryukyu Kempo, under Master Dillman. Thomas' work was first published in *Black Belt* in 1981. Since that time, numerous other articles have appeared in magazines in the U.S. and abroad.

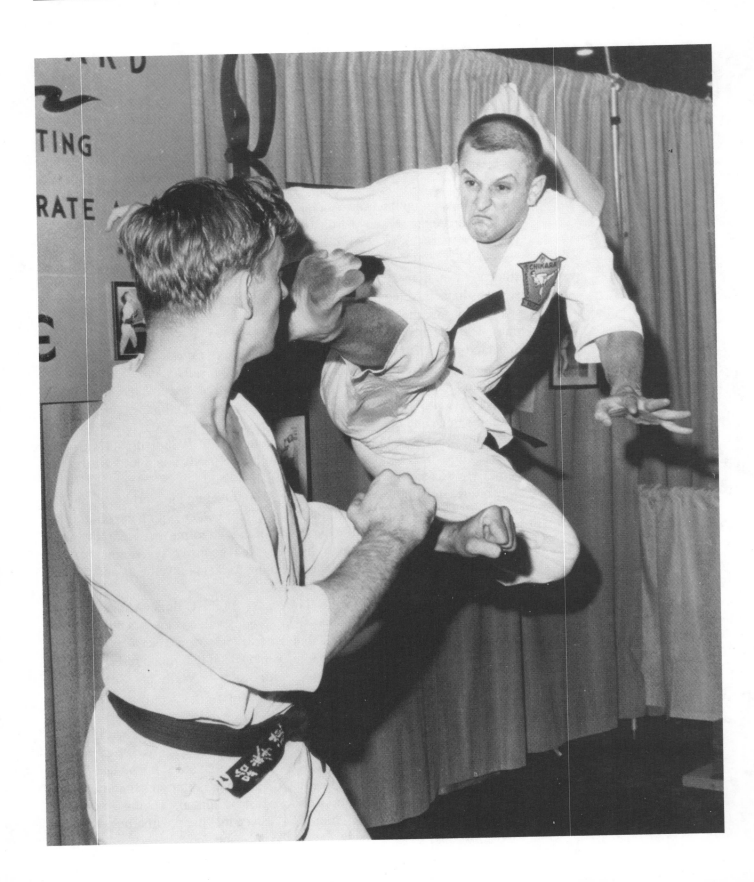

**Left page:** In 1966, The International Sports Show at Washington, D.C. featured 1st Lt. (army), Military Police Commander George A. Dillman as a main feature. Here he places a flying kick on the nose of a 6'3" opponent.

**Top left:** George A. Dillman, demonstrates arm and throat attacking on Kimberly "Fritz" Dillman for a special film *Self-defense for Women: A Positive Approach* made for CBS films.
Photo by R.B. Romanski, Reading Eagle Newspaper, May 1970.

**Top right:** George A. Dillman, touted as the "winningest Black Belt" that karate has ever known—by Official Karate Magazine—won 327 trophies in fighting, form, weapons, breaking and demonstration.
Photo by J.R. Cutler, Reading Eagle, June 1970.

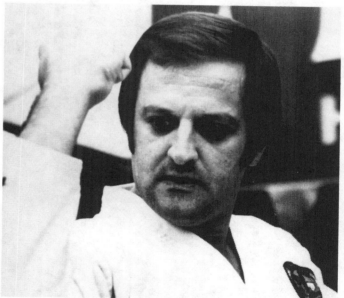

**Left page:** George A. Dillman, III instructs his son George, IV in the art of karate as the Dillman team prepares for a tournament competition and demonstration. On the floor taking the punch is the youngest Dillman (age 5) Allen.
Photo by Ralph Jenkins, 1970

**Top left:** Allen B. Dillman, flying high in his youth—easily breaks boards.

**Top right:** George A. Dillman, (right) does a pressure point knock-out on Black Belt Tom Muncy of Virginia (Tom is 6'4" and 240lbs)

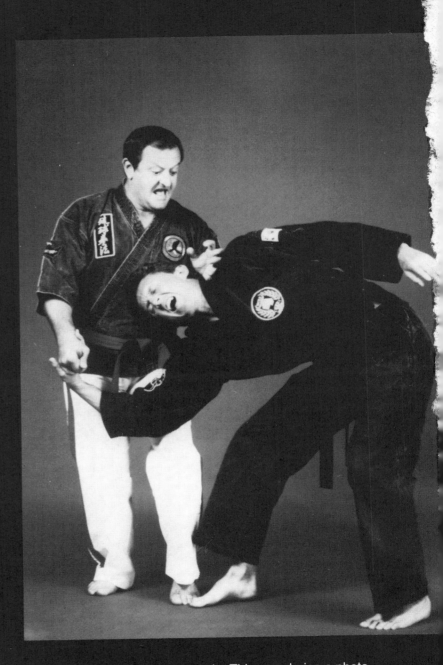

**Top left:** George A. Dillman knocks out Len Gambla with a pressure point attack to the neck. This was during a photo shoot for Black Belt magazine. Dillman has been featured on numerous magazine covers and featured over 100 times in the past three decades.
Photo by Doug Churchill

**Top right:** Dillman uses "small circle" theory on the finger and attacks the neck of Ian Waite of New Zealand.
Photo by Doug Churchill

George A. Dillman breaks big blocks of ice. This has earned him much national publicity.

**Top:** Remy Presas, George Dillman and Wally Jay (1991) at the open house for Dillman Karate International in Reading, Pennsylvania.

**Top right:** Left to right: Kimberly F. Dillman, Ralph Jenkins, George A. Dillman, Sandra L. Schlessman. Dillman Karate International, Reading, Pa.

**Bottom right:** These are some of the Black Belts who attended the Dillman Karate International open house weekend, Nov. 23, 1991.  A total of 153 attended from 17 states.

**Top:** Dillman seminar tour (left to right): Jerry Smith, Greg Dillon, Will Higginbotham, George A. Dillman, Jim Corn. The Dillman team has traveled the USA by motor coach teaching and sharing his studies with all that will listen. Photo by K. Dillman

**Bottom:** George A. Dillman talks with seminar participants and answers their many questions on his theory of pressure point fighting.

George A. Dillman shatters ice in front of "Ripley's" museum on Fisherman's Wharf, San Francisco, CA for a world's record and main feature of *Ripley's Believe It or Not.*

# VIDEOS BY GEORGE A. DILLMAN—PRESSURE POINT INSTRUCTION:

**Tape 1:** Hidden pressure points, grappling, breakdown of common movements. ( 70 min.)

**Tape 2:** Kata Seiuchin- Dillman Theory breakdown of this deadly form. (70 min.)

**Tape 3:** Pinan Katas 1-4: Hard-hitting breakdown, grappling and use of hidden pressure point techniques. (70 min.)

**Tape 4:** Stances, Footwork, Power, Eye and Hand Coordination. Pressure points of the foot and leg. (70 min.)

**Tape 5:** Healing Tape. Learn how to correct the energy flow you disrupted during the practice of the Dillman Theories. (60 min.)

**Tape 6:** Advanced Pressure Points. Learn the correct angle and direction of strikes. Graphically displayed on a live model. Nai Hanchi Kata . (104 min.)

**Tape 7:** Live Seminar—filmed in New Orleans. 4 hours of seminar action edited to 60 minutes of pure instruction. Includes tuite and nerve strikes.

**Tape 8:** Bassai—filmed live. Learn knockouts, angle and direction. An exceptionally advanced detailed tape. ( 120 min. )

**Tape 9:** Personally Preferred Pressure Points— filmed live. Dillman and his students teach favorite techniques taken from katas. Includes 6 knockouts. (60 min.)

**Tape 10:** Dynamic Pressure Points—an advanced seminar on pressure points. Includes an explanation of the body's electrical system; attacks to head, legs, trunk; and how to incorporate Dillman theory into your classes. (120 min.)

**Tape 11:** Kata Bunkai—filmed live. Includes pressure point techniques from Kusanku, Chinto, Empi, and the Pinans. Learn triple-striking a single point, and the anatomy of the one-inch punch. 4 knockouts. ( 60 min.)

## OTHER VIDEO INSTRUCTION

**Tape A:** Breaking—Instruction on how to break, explained and demonstrated. Materials include wood and cement. ( 90 min.)

**Tape B:** Dillman Demo Team—Actual live demo by George Dillman and his team. A companion tape to the Breaking tape, showing the breaking techniques in action. ( 60 min.)

**Tape C:** 1985 Masters Show—A two hour show that brought the house down. Packed with exciting demonstrations by well-known martial artists. ( 60 min. )

**Tape D:** The Bo—Weapons Kata. Dillman performs and teaches three forms. Also includes demonstrations of kama, nunchaku, sai, and tonfa with a short history of each weapon. (60 min.)

**Left:** Mark Marshall, 270 lbs, goes out with the touch of George Dillman's hands.

**Right:** George A. Dillman touches pressure points and knocks out much larger opponents. Steve Jorgensen is out!
Photo by Kim Dillman, in New Zealand.

# GEORGE A. DILLMAN PERFORMANCES!

The Silverdome—Pontiac, MI

Veterans Stadium—Philadelphia, PA

The Spectrum—Philadelphia, PA

JFK Stadium—Washington, D.C.

Baltimore Stadium—Baltimore, MD

West Palm Beach Civic Center—West Palm Beach, FL

Ripley's Believe It or Not Museum—Fisherman's Wharf, San Francisco, CA

Reading Municipal Stadium—Reading, PA

Jackie Gleason Theatre—Miami Beach, FL

Performances were given along with the Dillman Karate Demonstration team, and drew standing ovations from packed-house crowds attending major events.

**Top left:** Jack Hogan (left), with just two fingers, knocks out a willing volunteer using the pressure points theory of George Dillman of Reading, Pa.

**Top right:** William O. Higginbotham (left) with a wrist grab and one touch knock-out.

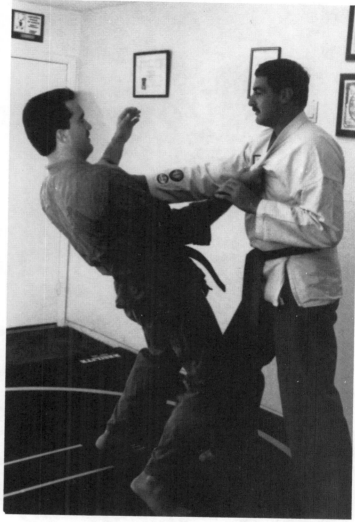

**Top left:** Rick Moneymaker, of Virginia, uses pressure points to tap out his opponent. Moneymaker has his own seminar following around the USA.

**Top right:** Mike Solecki, with "DKI" over twenty years, performs a "pressure point" attack on Jack Butler.

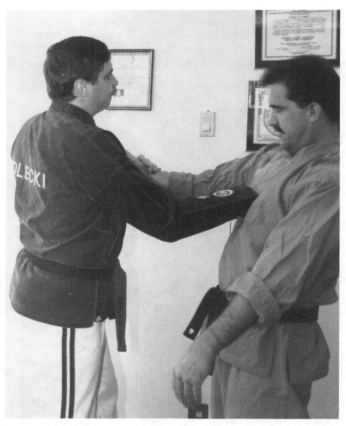

**Top left:** Sandra Schlessman (right), a former 5-year women's fighting champion demonstrates a pressure point attack to Tony Vargas.

**Top right:** Mike Solecki (left) performs a "pressure point" knock-out at his school in East Brunswick, NJ.

**Right page:** Rick Clark, 7th dan, knocks out much larger opponent during a seminar tour using the Dillman theory of pressure point attacking.

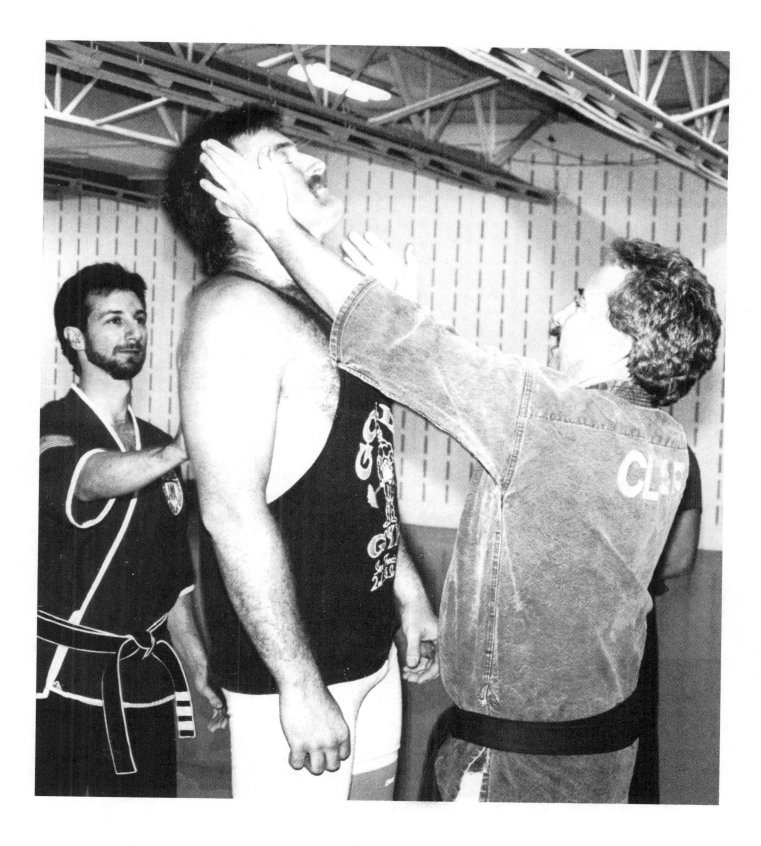

**Top left:** Bob "Pitt Bull" Golden does a pressure point knock-out on an opponent.
Photo by Jim Duncan

**Bottom left:** William O. Higginbotham, demonstrates a leg trap from a kata step and uses fingers for the knock-out.

**Top:** Tom Muncy puts out Pete Howell; Rick Moneymaker catches. Moneymaker and Muncy have been with the Dillman Theory from the beginning and helped with research.

# WARNING

This is an educational book,
but these techniques are
NOT TO BE PERFORMED WITHOUT
PROPER SUPERVISION.
We want to share our years of
experience with you, but we do not
want anyone injured.
It is essential that you consult
a physician regarding
whether or not to attempt any
technique shown in this book.
Always have a
Dillman Method instructor
supervise your practice.

# Table of Contents

琉球拳法

# INTRODUCTION

When westerners first heard of the oriental martial arts, we were enchanted by stories of almost magical abilities. These stories entranced and enthralled, and became the impetus for many to begin martial arts training. After a short time, however, it began to seem that those wondrous abilities did not really exist at all, that they were just a figment of our desire for invincibility.

Part of the reason for this was that great martial arts skill resulted from years of rigorous training, far more than most were willing to invest. And some of what appeared so wondrous was simply novelty. A person who has boxed, but never worked with a martial artist will be amazed to be kicked at will. After learning to throw and counter kicks, the boxer's amazement disappears.

Yet, a portion of the martial arts mystique still remained—some element of the wondrous which could not be dismissed as the result of years of sweat, or the consequence of novelty. There remained an elusive element which lay at the heart of the mythology created by the oriental masters.

No one seemed to be able to do what the legendary masters could do. The stories were there, but the knowledge was lacking. It meant that either we, as western martial artists, had been duped, or something was being held back. It is our contention that vital knowledge has been withheld from us, the knowledge of pressure points and their purpose as applied in the arts of *kyusho-jitsu* (striking pressure points) and *tuite* or *torite* (using pressure points for joint manipulation). We also believe that this knowledge is fully contained in the formal exercises (kata) of the martial arts.

The irony of this situation is incredible; most karate practitioners holding first degree black belts know anywhere from eight to eighteen kata. Several styles contain literally dozens of kata, and there are practitioners who can perform them all, yet have no idea what they contain. They have flawless performance, but no comprehension. In this way, western karate practitioners can be compared to a choir singing in a foreign language. They may sing the notes perfectly but they do not understand the meaning of the words.

We feel that western martial artists have trained in the dark long enough. It is time for fluent movement to give way to genuine understanding and comprehension. It is to this purpose that we present this material. It is our hope that having some insight into what we truly possess will motivate all our fellow martial artists to a more sincere and diligent study of the arts we value.

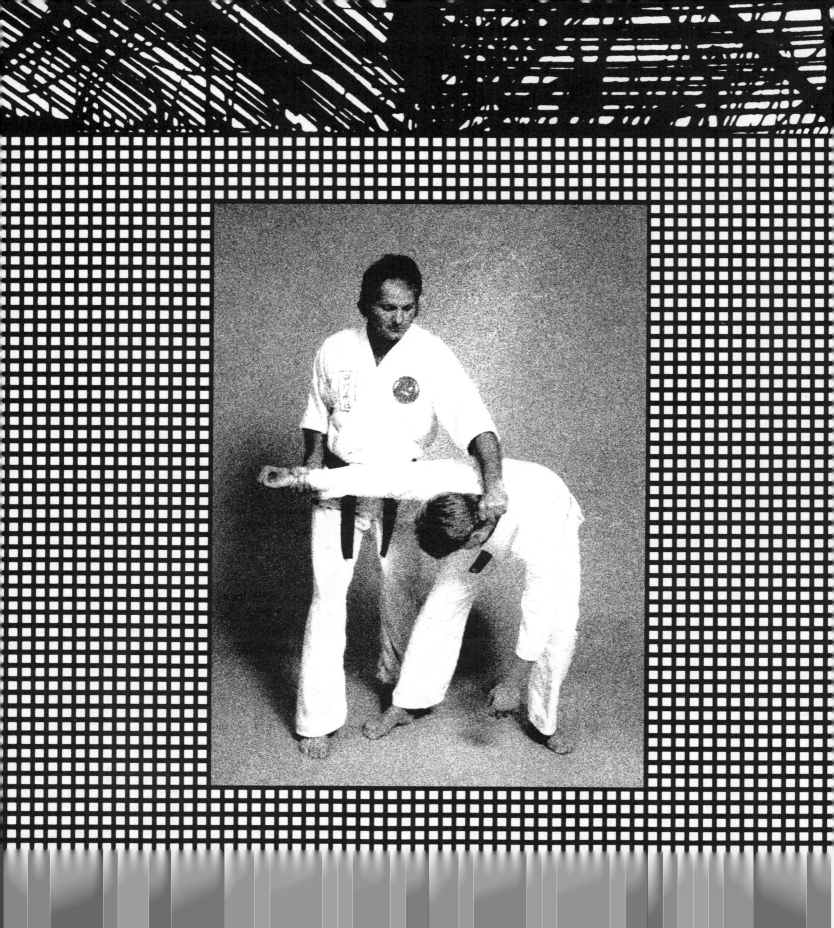

# KARATE & RYUKYU KEMPO

Karate is a household word.  The average person hears the word karate and thinks, "Oh, *karotty*.  That's fighting with kicks and chops."  To the karate-ka, on the other hand, karate is the art of self-defense which evolved in Okinawa, based on indigenous Okinawan methods blended with Chinese kung-fu.  However, most karate-ka are thinking of *karate-do* when they hear the word karate.  Karate-do is an art of this century.  It is the modern incarnation of an older art called Ryukyu kempo to-de (or karate) jitsu (which roughly translates as Okinawan kung-fu, Chinese boxing science).

In fact, the name karate, as we know it, did not really exist until about 1930.  At that time certain Ryukyu kempo teachers sought to popularize the art among the Japanese.  They felt that eliminating the Chinese reference in the old name would be more palatable to the nationalistic sensibilities of pre-WW II imperial Japan.

Karate-do is a modified, popularist version of Ryukyu kempo.  It was shaped by the great forces of the day which acted to save traditional martial arts from extinction by converting them into "ways of enlightenment".
The path was already well beaten by kenjutsu and jujitsu.  Kenjutsu, or samurai sword fighting, had been watered down into kendo — fencing.  Jujitsu, or samurai hand-to-hand combat, had been diluted into judo.

The transformation of kenjutsu to kendo was made by eliminating danger and combative realism, and replacing them with protective equipment and competitions.  Kendo substituted the sword with the bamboo shinai, covered the players in armor and reduced sword fighting's myriad techniques to four cuts, one thrust and four legal targets.  Jujitsu eliminated deadly striking

**Left:** Steve Gould, demonstrates wrist grappling and points to attack on opponent's neck and head, opposite side.

techniques, as well as the most dangerous throws, and adopted rules for safe contests to bring judo into being, thus creating a popular wrestling-type sport. Though these arts retained some element of combative effectiveness, the most deadly and battle-proven portions were eliminated.

Karate-do followed suit. To enhance the value of the training for self-improvement, techniques and kata were altered, making them more aesthetic and expansive. The modern art can be used with effectiveness in self-defense, but it is primarily designed for self-development and sporting competition. It is a safe, rule-governed game with the most effective and deadly aspects dissected. In short, karate-philosophy took precedence over combat.

This is not a bad thing. Karate in its present form is a safe and beneficial practice for millions around the world. It is simply not the combat art it was. And since many people begin martial arts training to learn self-defense, karate is often not the art they expected. But, it would be misleading to conclude that what is needed is merely a return to older methods of performance. Some might assume that if they simply could do a kata the way it was performed in 1900, rather than the way it is performed today, that they would suddenly be practicing old-style Ryukyu kempo. This is simply not true.

The essence of Ryukyu kempo does not lie in the technical performance of some kata or movement (though, as we shall discuss, there are some important technical distinctions). The essence of Ryukyu kempo lies in its understanding of what particular movements and actions represent. It is meaning, not performance that makes the art what it is. **The meaning of Ryukyu kempo is pressure point fighting: Kyusho-jitsu.** And the information about pressure points is contained and revealed in kata.

Pressure point fighting is a precise art. It requires an exact knowledge of the location and use of small targets on the body. Different points have different functions. Different points work together in different ways. And points cannot usually be activated head-on. Each has a particular angle at which it must be struck or pressed to produce results. Yet, in a fight there is no time to think about where a pressure point is, or which points correspond.

In the practice of kata, the location and inter-relationship of various points are rehearsed. Some of the kata movements represent the opponent's actions. Some show exactly the movement the defender makes, and some techniques show, on the performer's body, the points to be struck on an attacker's body. All of this means that the most important part of the kata practice is the mental component of picturing the attacker and the vital points.

This is why karate masters have always stressed the need for visualization during kata practice. And this is why the old masters took longer to perform a kata than the modern student. The modern student rushes through the form to show the athletic perfection attained. The masters of old were too busy practicing the full *meaning* of the form—not merely its physical expression—to hurry the movements.

Mental rehearsal combined and reinforced by physical rehearsal through kata practice makes instantaneous use of pressure point knowledge possible. In this way the Ryukyu kempo exponent programs the subconscious mind to actually use the techniques effectively. This does not mean that other common types of martial arts training, such as basics and sparring, are unnecessary. But, it does mean that kata is truly the very heart of traditional combat-oriented martial arts training, just as we were told.

It also means that the modern karate student who wishes to reclaim the value of the original karate art does not need to learn different kata. For the most part, the traditional kata practiced in any dojo are fine. These already contain valuable pressure point information; it is simply a matter of recognition. But, this also means that modern martial artists have had pressure point information at their disposal all along, and never knew it. The reason is that kata also conceals information.

The concealment of information has always been a part of the martial arts. In China, most styles originated as family systems, taught only to family members. When the scope of students was expanded to include a whole village, some teaching was held back, reserved solely for the immediate family.

In traditional Japanese bujutsu (the warrior arts of the samurai) instruction was divided into three levels. There was *shoden*, or basic teaching, *chuden*, or intermediate teaching, and *okuden*, or secret teaching. Only a very few were entrusted with the okuden material. Everyone else was deliberately excluded.

In Okinawa, martial arts training was conducted in secret, usually late at night. Because the training was secret, hard to obtain, and sometimes illegal, it was highly valued. Teachers usually tested prospective students to make sure that they were worthy to learn. These tests often consisted of periods of time given over to chores or menial tasks having no relationship to karate. Sometimes the tests consisted of months performing one stance, or a single basic technique with no explanation, little correction, and less acknowledgement.

In this setting, a beginning student might have been performing a basic stepping action in the same room as senior students who were working on their advanced kata. How was the instructor to prevent the beginner—not yet deemed worthy to receive deep training—from picking up the secrets of the art? The answer lay in the misleading nature of kata.

It is not possible to look at a kata and see what is really going on, unless one is trained in the deepest aspects of the art. In meaning, kata movements change point of view constantly—one moment showing the attack, the next showing the defense. The kata itself follows a particular sequence, yet, this often has no relationship to the sequence to be used in a fight. The performance of kata is continuous, but the meaning is interpreted in smaller units. The directions of movements in kata steps may appear to represent the direction from which various attacks originate, when in fact they tell the practitioner at what angle to position himself in relation to the attacker.

The effectiveness of this misleading quality was fully evident in the interpretation which westerners gave to karate kata when they were first exposed to it. In post-war Japan, the occupying U.S. military banned the practice of traditional Japanese martial arts, including judo and kendo. But, karate practice was allowed because the American authorities did not recognize the combative essence of kata practice. To them it was merely a traditional martial dance, or, at most, shadow-boxing.

In 1906 Ryukyu kempo was, for the first time, taught openly, by the legendary Anko Itosu. Itosu was teaching school children. The emphasis in this instruction was discipline and physical well being, not combat, so the art was taught with even greater concealment. In fact, the art began to be taught incorrectly. The children were told, "This is a block against a front kick," and "Always make sure to block with your wrist." They were told, "Make sure to fold your thumb past your middle finger when making a fist," and, "Twist your fist all the way over when punching."

These misrepresentations of Ryukyu kempo served the dual purpose of protecting the children from unintentional injury, and making certain that secrets were kept from students whose character had not been fully tested. But, the students were not told that they were being misled, so when they themselves began to teach they did not realize they were teaching inaccurately.

The misrepresentation of Ryukyu kempo was further aggravated by racial bias. The Okinawan people have always regarded themselves as culturally and racially distinct from the Japanese, even though politically speaking Okinawa has been a part of Japan since the 1700's (Okinawa was separated from Japan for a period of time following WW II). When Ryukyu kempo was first introduced to Japan, it was taught largely as it was practiced in Okinawa. This can be seen in Gichin Funakoshi's (the "father of Japanese karate") early book, <u>Ryukyu Kempo Karate</u>. However, within a decade, material was being removed and changed, and Japanese students were learning a different art.

Evidence of this divergence is easily documented. For example, early photos of Funakoshi demonstrating karate almost always show him to have grabbed his opponent with one hand while striking with the other. But, modern books on karate, as well as later Japanese instructors, almost never mention grasping the opponent. Rather, they teach that the non-punching hand should be pulled strongly back to the hip. It is of even greater significance to observe that in those demonstrations, Funakoshi can be seen to be grabbing *pressure points*, a subject completely absent from most modern karate instruction.

If the Okinawans were reluctant to reveal their martial secrets to the Japanese, how much more would they be unwilling to show westerners. Americans are *gaijin*, foreigners, barbarians.

When Americans appeared on Okinawa it was in the form of an invading army and occupying forces. How likely is it that anybody would teach invaders their self-defense secrets? When American soldiers became interested in studying karate, the Okinawans taught them the watered-down school children's art. In this way, modern American students became the inheritors of karate-do, the art the Okinawans were willing to share openly. But, kyusho-jitsu, the art of pressure point fighting, was held back. And so, we have two distinct, though related systems. One is the modern, athletic, competitive, popular art of karate-do. The other is the secret, traditional and deadly fighting art of Ryukyu kempo.

# TECHNICAL DISTINCTIONS

For the most part, the physical movements of Ryukyu kempo and those of karate are the same. The difference is one of meaning and interpretation, more than technique. However, there are some ways in which Ryukyu kempo differs in performance from the popularly taught karate methods. We believe that these variances are due to Ryukyu kempo weapons being "blunted" for safety's sake in public karate classes.

**Left:** Mike Patton (left) with his instructor George A. Dillman. Patton was one of the first teaching true Okinawan Kempo Karate in Ohio, and had five schools in the N-W corner of the state.

## TEGATA or SHUTO: SWORD HAND

(1) In popular karate, the common open hand formation is taught with the fingers arched, the palm pressed forward and the thumb tucked.
(2) However, in this position, the technique does not work. The arched fingers cannot be used in a spear hand technique to dig into the target, instead they fold, preventing penetration .
(3) The little finger gives way when the hand is used in a chopping fashion so that the impact is dulled.

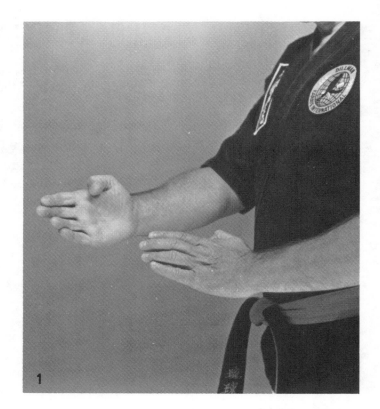

2

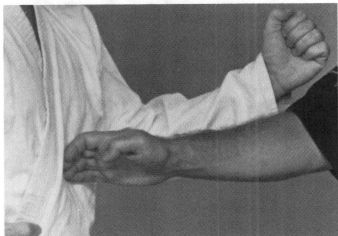

close-up

continued

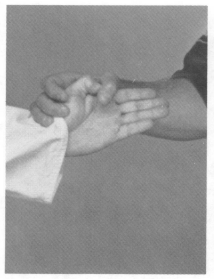

close-up

4

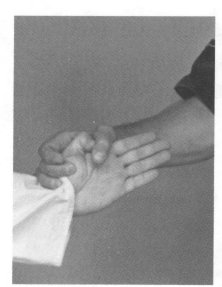

close-up

5

## TEGATA or SHUTO: SWORD HAND

*Continued from previous page*

(4 & 5) And the tucked thumb is a joint lock waiting to be applied.

(6) In Ryukyu kempo, the open hand is formed differently. The fingers are held straight, with the little finger rolled in towards the palm. The thumb is also straight and on the inside, so that the back of the hand is rounded and the palm is slightly cupped.

(7) The stiffened fingers can dig strongly into pressure points. The side of the hand is strengthened for striking, and the thumb is protected. Also, the form of the hand, with the palm cupped, is the same as a technique known in taijiquan as the "willow leaf hand." This position is especially good in the application of ki (or chi = "vital energy") which is said to pool in the palm.

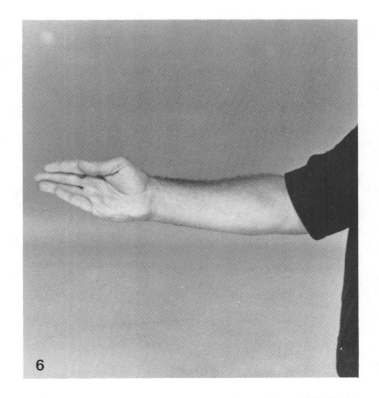

6

7

## SEIKEN: BASIC FIST

(1) In much of the popular karate instruction, the student is told, when forming a fist, to fold the thumb tightly over the first two fingers.

(2) In Ryukyu kempo the thumb does not extend past the first finger, which is kept straight at the last knuckle. This is because reaching too far with the thumb stretches and weakens the back of the hand, making for a less solid fist.

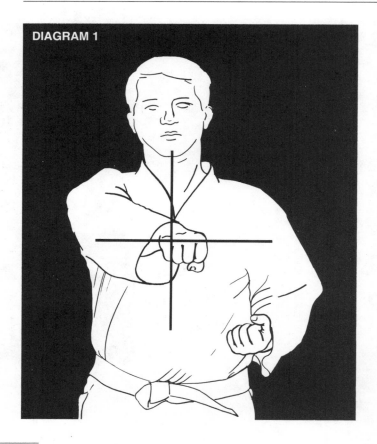

## 3/4 TWIST PUNCH

The most significant difference between popular karate and Ryukyu kempo is the method of punching.

(1) In karate, the punch begins with the fist placed, palm up, on the hip.

(2 & 3) Then as the punch is executed, the fist turns to a palm down position directly in the center-line of the body (DIAGRAM 1).

DIAGRAM 1

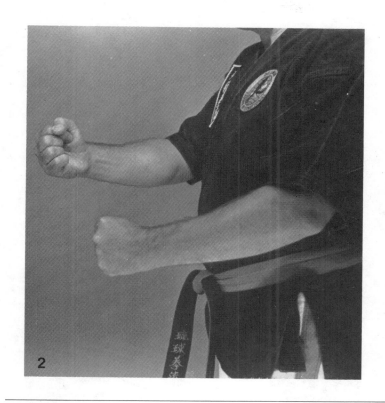

47

continued

## 3/4 TWIST PUNCH

*Continued from previous page*

(4 & 5) The Ryukyu kempo punch begins the same way, but rotates only 3/4th's of a turn, ending with the fist just past vertical and off center slightly (DIAGRAM 2). At the end of the punch, the wrist also flexes slightly, to increase the transfer of energy into the target (DIAGRAM 3).

The 3/4 punch is superior to the full twist punch for several reasons:

1. The 3/4 punch is skeletally stronger. As the full twist punch rotates, the two bones of the forearm, the ulna and the radius, criss-cross each other (DIAGRAM 4). In the 3/4 punch, the bones are actually aligned straight, with no cross-over (DIAGRAM 5).

2. In the full twist punch, the muscles of the forearm (the extensor carpi radialis longus and the brachioradialis) are stretched passed the point of maximum efficiency. Since these muscles also reinforce the wrist, the technique is weakened, and the fist is more likely to buckle. (6) In the 3/4 punch, however, the muscles are at the point of maximum efficiency. This means the wrist will be better supported on impact, and more capable of transferring energy into the target.

DIAGRAM 2

DIAGRAM 3

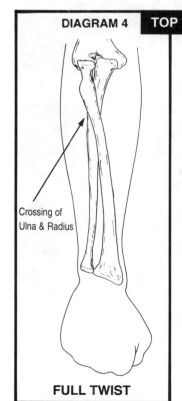

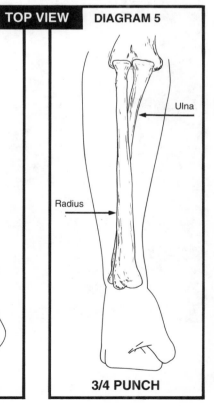

DIAGRAM 4 **TOP VIEW** DIAGRAM 5

Crossing of
Ulna & Radius

Ulna

Radius

**FULL TWIST**

**3/4 PUNCH**

## 3/4 TWIST PUNCH

*Continued from previous page*

3. The full twist punch is not a natural body position. This is why beginners tend to flop their elbows and rotate their shoulders when learning the technique.

(7)The 3/4 punch, however, is perfectly natural and comfortable. (In fact, compare the position of the fist at the completion of 3/4 punch with the position of hands on a steering wheel).

4. In the full twist punch, the alignment of the fist on impact does not correspond to the natural shape of the body. Force is spread over a larger area and focused penetration is reduced. In contrast, the 3/4 punch perfectly matches the natural angles of the body, allowing precise focus and concentration of power (DIAGRAM 6 & 6A)

*It is easy to see how the full twist punch, by being unnatural, structurally weak, and misaligned on impact, would provide a safer method for students to practice. It is also clear how the 3/4 punch is the more effective for combat.*

7

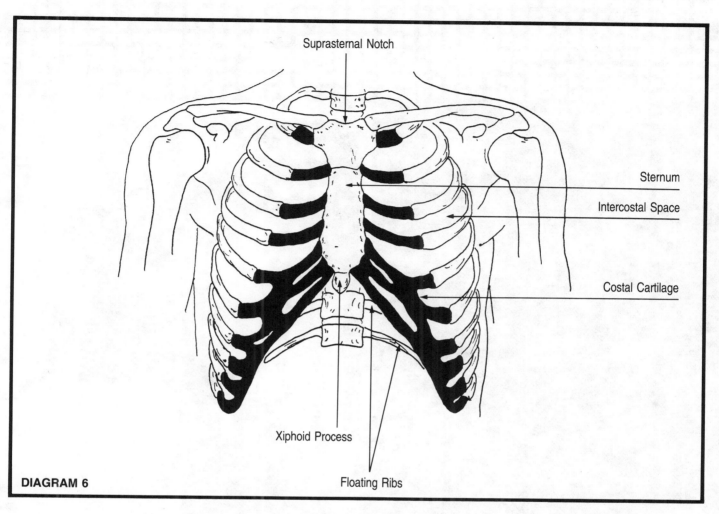

Suprasternal Notch

Sternum

Intercostal Space

Costal Cartilage

Xiphoid Process

Floating Ribs

**DIAGRAM 6**

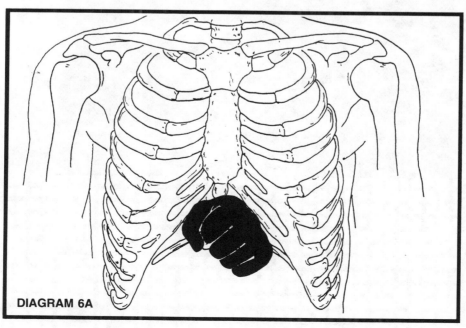

**DIAGRAM 6A**

# PRESSURE POINTS

In general terms, a pressure point is a place where energy can be transmitted most effectively into a nerve. It is usually a place where there is a small branch of nerve connecting two or more major nerve pathways, or a place where major nerves join together (a nerve plexus). This means that when such an area is struck, the pain signal registers on more than one nerve pathway. Pain entered into a pressure point on the arm, for example, might be carried to the brain on all three major nerves of the arm — the radial, medial and ulnar nerves. This is why kyusho-jitsu requires less power to be effective; the brain receives a signal which is amplified by the multiple nerve routes.

The pressure points used in kyusho-jitsu are the same points used in acupuncture. For this reason, acupuncture theories can also describe how kyusho-jitsu works. Acupuncture regards a pressure point as a gate where the flow of vital energy (chi or ki) can be manipulated. The acupuncturist uses these gates to increase or decrease the flow of energy in order to restore a healthful balance within the body system. The kyusho-jitsu fighter uses the same points to disrupt the flow of energy in order to defeat the opponent.

According to acupuncture theory, pressure points lie on pathways, called meridians which are associated with certain organs of the body. Acupuncturists maintain that stimulating a point has a direct effect on the condition of the corresponding organ. There are fourteen meridians, twelve of which are found on both the right and left sides of the body (bilateral). The last two are on the body centerline. These meridians are named for the organ with which they correspond. They are: 1. Stomach; 2. Spleen; 3. Gall Bladder; 4. Liver; 5. Urinary Bladder; 6. Kidney; 7. Heart; 8. Small Intestine; 9. Lung; 10. Large Intestine; 11. Pericardium (sometimes called "Governor of the Heart"); 12. Triple Warmer (sometimes called "Thyroid"); 13. Governor (on the back centerline, corresponding to the spinal column); 14. Conception (on the front centerline, corresponding to the genitals and the tanden, the source of ki).

**Left:** George A. Dillman watches as David Hogan (left) proves that a child can use the "Pressure Point" Theory that he teaches. Adrian Shepperd, on the right, is a 200-lb plus black belt from the Martial Arts Academy in Jacksonville, Florida.

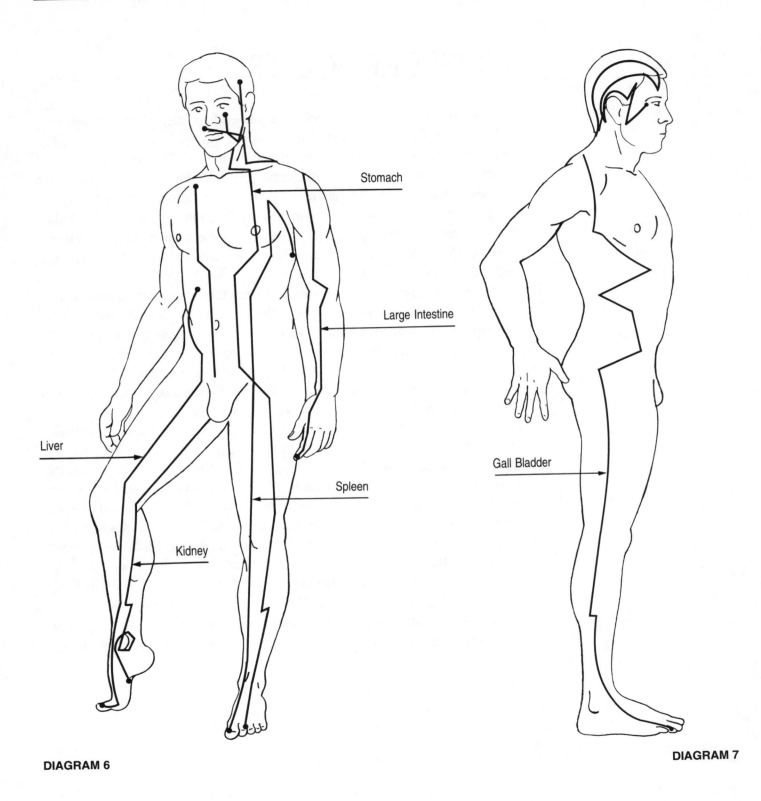

Stomach

Large Intestine

Liver

Spleen

Kidney

Gall Bladder

**DIAGRAM 6**

**DIAGRAM 7**

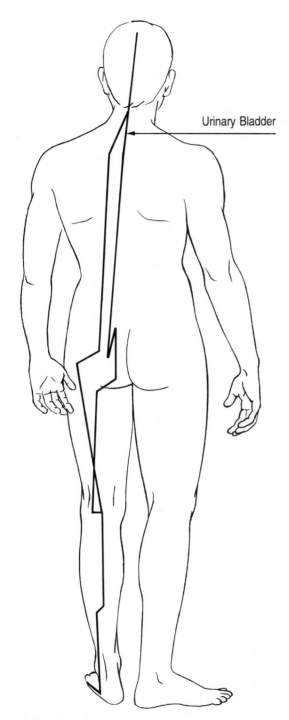

**DIAGRAM 8**

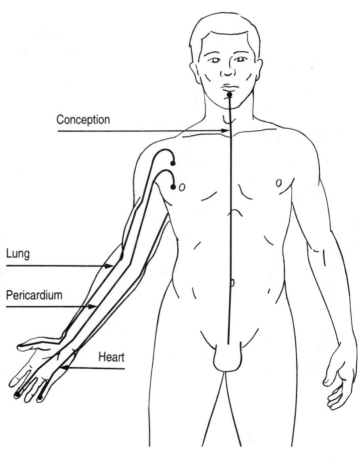

Urinary Bladder

Conception

Lung

Pericardium

Heart

**DIAGRAM 9**

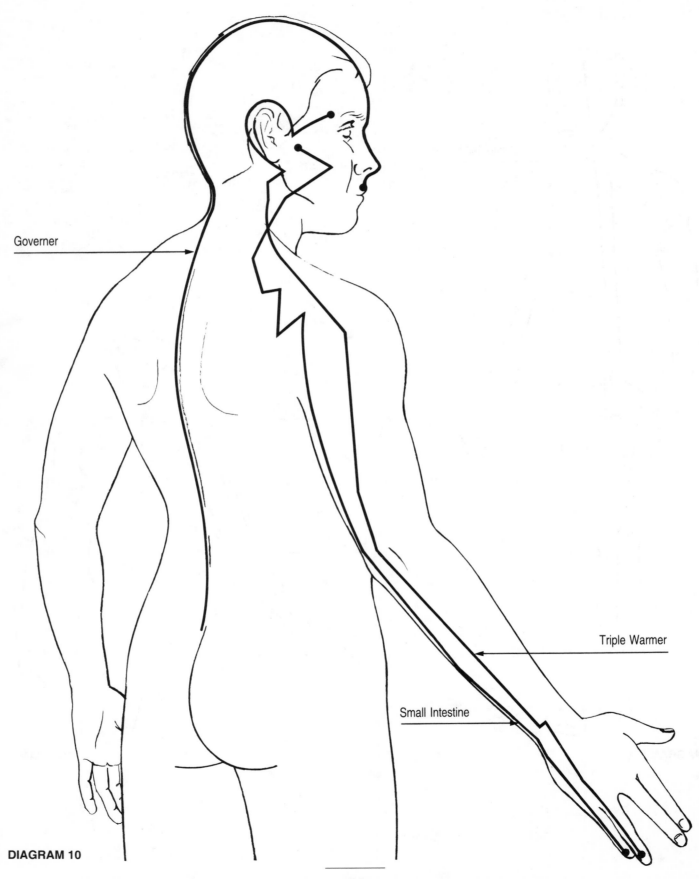

Governer

Triple Warmer

Small Intestine

**DIAGRAM 10**

Since the original founders of pressure point combat were forced to use these methods against armed assailants, their techniques were intended to kill. They used the points to stop the function of their opponents' organs. Stopping the heart, for example, would cause immediate death. Stopping the kidneys or liver would result in death after a few days. This is, we believe, the source for the legends concerning the "death touch" and the "delayed death touch."

In modern kyusho-jitsu practice our goal is to defend ourselves and not to kill; therefore, our techniques emphasize quickly incapacitating an opponent with a knock-out or joint attack. We also take the wisdom of acupuncture seriously in our own training, and use the utmost restraint in practicing our pressure point techniques. We do not indiscriminately strike points, lest we inadvertently affect the function of a training partner's organs.

Just as we would never poke someone in the eye to see if that is an effective self-defense technique, we also never train full power and full contact on pressure points. This is simply common sense. In practice we only tap very lightly on points. This method is best because it insures that no one is injured, and helps us to train for accuracy of technique (the lighter the blow, the more precise it must be to register).

We are also careful not to do pressure point work for extended training sessions. Rather, we limit ourselves to only about fifteen minutes per week. The majority of the time, we only indicate the strike. We also administer an "energy restoration" technique (kuatsu, see below) anytime we tap a point.

As for the reader, our advice is to find an instructor of this art to supervise your training. **We do not recommend trying to learn this art on your own. If you choose to attempt the techniques described in the book, then use restraint. Do not strike head or neck points at all.** If you decide to strike an arm point, only hit as hard as if knocking on a door. If your partner begins to feel nauseous, dizzy or short of breath it means you have been working the points too long. These symptoms will pass shortly if you stop practicing. It will also help to have someone administer a general energy restoration technique (method # 2, below).

There are different types of pressure points, defined by how they are activated. Some are activated by striking, some by pushing or pressing, and others by rubbing. It is important to know which type of point is which. Further, the angle at which a point is attacked is important. Though striking a pressure point at the wrong angle may have some result, the full effect cannot be realized unless the point is pressed or struck correctly.

The basic theory of pressure point fighting is this: Striking one point causes pain. Striking or pressing two points at the same time causes the effect to be registered in the middle. Sometimes this means the pain itself is referred to a place between the two points. Sometimes the physical reaction to the pain manifests itself at the mid-point, even though the victim experiences two distinct sources of pain.

Working against three vital points at the same time results in unconsciousness, with a 99.9% chance of revival. There are a few places on the body where one hand can activate three points, but generally a three point knock-out requires both hands working together, or two consecutive movements of one hand to accomplish.

Attacking four vital points will disrupt a major organ (which organ depends on the meridians being worked) resulting in unconsciousness leading to death if resuscitation is not applied. However, there is a 90% chance of reviving the victim using energy restoration techniques.

Striking or pressing five coordinated vital points in the correct manner and sequence is fatal.

Because of the obvious danger of simply playing around with pressure points, the following rules of training must be strictly observed.

1. Train only under a qualified instructor.

2. Do not practice actually striking on pressure points for more than fifteen minutes per week.

3. When training, do not switch sides. Only strike on one side of the body in any given training session.

4. Do not apply cross-body techniques, that is, do not strike corresponding points on opposite sides of your partner's body.

5. Be sure to learn proper revival techniques.

6. Do not work pressure points on persons with health problems, or people over the age of 40, or people on drugs (legal or otherwise).

7. Use the utmost restraint at all times. It is not necessary to fully knock-out someone to see the effect of a pressure point. Usually a light blow is sufficient to demonstrate effectiveness.

## BASIC PRESSURE POINTS

The first—and in many ways the most important—pressure points are located on the arm. These are the first points taught because they are effective points while also being reasonably safe to practice on. Obviously, to learn pressure point work requires supervised hands-on training. To begin on body or head points would be tremendously foolhardy. Familiarity must be learned in a controlled manner, and the arm-points allow for such a safe training ground.

However, that is not to say there is no risk in working arm points. And so, we must stress again the need for restraint, proper instruction and supervision in kyusho-jitsu practice. The meridians of the arm include the Heart and the Lung meridians. These internal organs are affected by working on the arm pressure points. For this reason, pressure point work should be limited to just 15 minutes a week. Further, these techniques should never be applied on persons with compromised health (especially heart or respiratory problems) or on those who are using drugs (legal or otherwise) which might effect these organs.

From a combative standpoint, the arm pressure points are essential because they are the most easily attacked targets. As an assailant reaches out with a strike or grab, the nerves of the arm are stretched by the extension of the limb and the tensing of muscles, making these arm points particularly vulnerable to attack. Generally, striking or pressing on the arm points causes some other target to become vulnerable. Therefore, the arm points are primarily used as set-up or entry points. However, it is possible to end a fight using only the arm points, so their value must not be underestimated.

## LOCATION OF ARM POINTS

Because the pressure points of kyusho-jitsu are the same as the points of acupuncture, we find it most convenient to refer to them using common acupuncture nomenclature. As explained above, the acupuncturists believe that ki (chi) flows through the body along pathways, called channels, or meridians. Pressure points lie on these pathways, and are numbered according to their position. The meridians themselves are named for the internal organ they are associated with. A pressure point is actually quite small, about the size of the tip of a ball-point ben. In kyusho-jitsu, however, the area of activation is about the size of a quarter (25¢ piece).

# POINTS ALONG THE INSIDE OF THE ARM

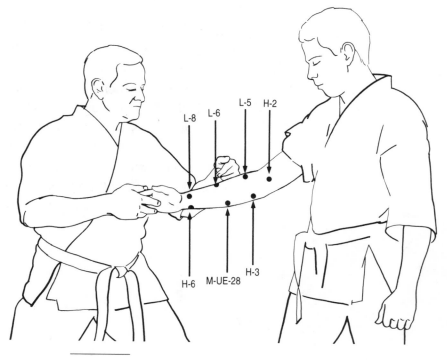

## HEART # 6

This is a touch-point located on the little finger side of the wrist, 1/2 inch from the wrist joint. It lies slightly toward the inside of the ulnar bone along the line of the ulnar nerve. This point controls energy to the wrist, and pressing it will weaken the wrist, making it easier to bend.

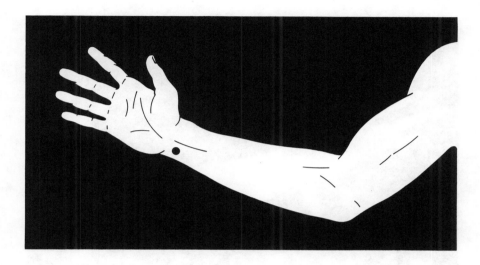

## LUNG # 8

This point is located on the thumb side of the wrist, directly up from H-6. It is a push point lying over the radial nerve and against the radius. This point controls the making of a fist. Catching this point while blocking can cause the fist to give way, greatly reducing its ability to transfer energy should the technique strike.

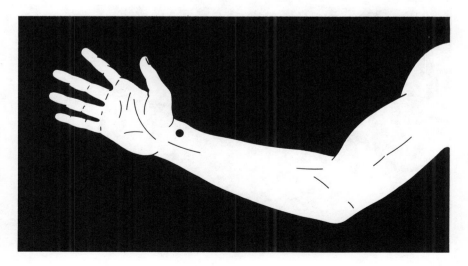

## LOWER MID-FOREARM POINT

This point lies on the heart meridian, about midway along the inner aspect of the ulna, directly down from L-6 (below). In acupuncture this is an "extraordinary point", sometimes designated as M-UE-28. It is a hit-point and controls the wrist.

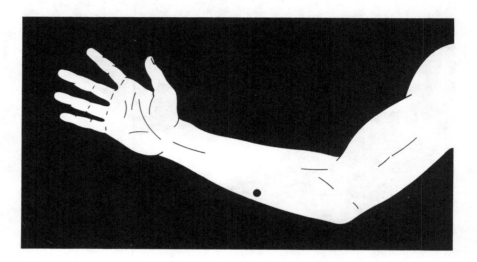

## LUNG # 6

This point is located at the end of the radiobrachialis muscle (the muscle on the thumb side of the forearm) along the inside of the arm. The length of the radiobrachialis varies among different people, so the location of this point can vary, but it is approximately in the mid-point of the forearm. This is a hit-point which controls the fist.

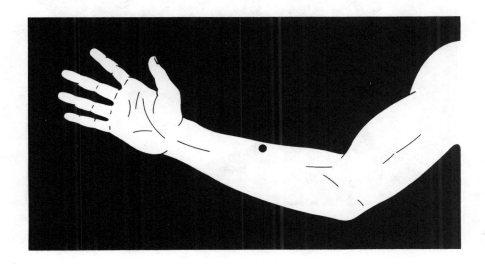

## LUNG # 5

This hit-point is located inside the forearm next to the radiobrachialis, about one inch down from the crease of the elbow. Striking this point will cause the knees to buckle, exposing the opposite leg to attack. In most individuals, striking this point while holding the wrist points will put the opponent on the ground.

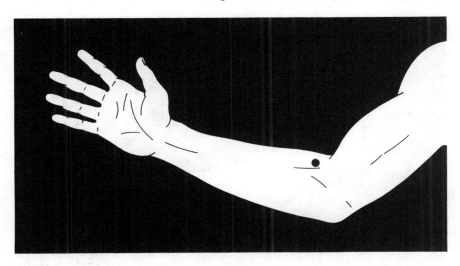

## HEART # 3

H-3 is just below the knob of the elbow on the inside of the arm. It may be struck or firmly pressed to bend the elbow.

## HEART # 2

H-2 is located on the inside of the arm, above the knob of the elbow.
H-2 actually represents both a specific point, and the area above the elbow on the inside of the triceps along the ulnar nerve and brachial artery (in fact, some acupuncture texts specify two points, designated H-2A & H-2B). A strike to this area can cause the arm to bend and the fingers to curl inward.

# POINTS ALONG THE OUTSIDE OF THE ARM

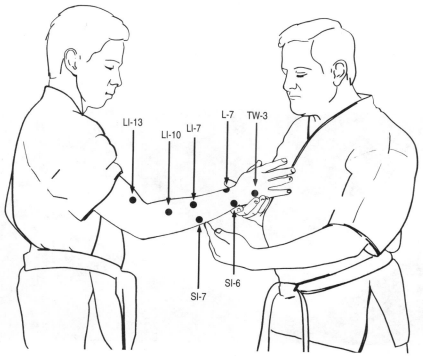

## TRIPLE WARMER # 3

This is a push-point, located on the back of the hand between the bones of the fourth and fifth fingers, one-third the distance from the knuckles to the wrist. This point is used in joint manipulation techniques against the wrist. Because the smaller bones of the hand are delicate, this can also be a hit-point.

**Note:** the Triple Warmer meridian is associated with the thyroid, an organ unknown to the ancient Chinese.

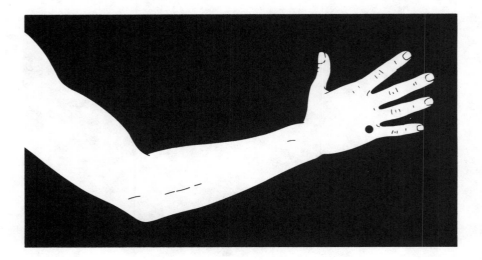

## SMALL INTESTINE # 6

This push-point is located on the outside of the arm (opposite H-6). It is at the base of the styloid process of the ulna at a dorsal branch of the ulnar nerve.

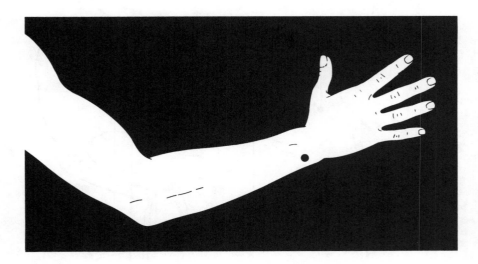

## LUNG # 7

This point lies directly on the top of the radius, about 1/2" up from L-8.
It responds to a rub and loosens the fist. When grabbing the wrist, this point
must be manipulated towards the outside of the radial bone.

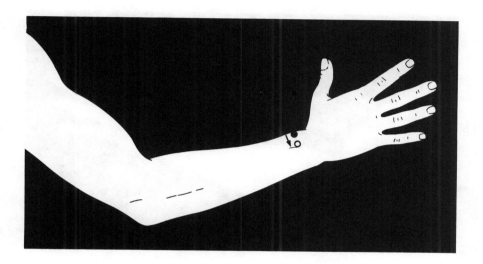

## LARGE INTESTINE # 7

This point lies on the outside of the radius, about the middle of the forearm. It is located opposite to L-6. It is at the end of the extensor carpi radialis brevis muscle.

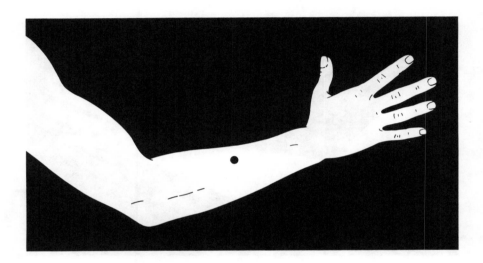

## SMALL INTESTINE # 7

This point is located on the outside of the ulna about midway along the forearm opposite to the Lower Mid-forearm Point (M-UE-28). Strike this point to release and bend the wrist.

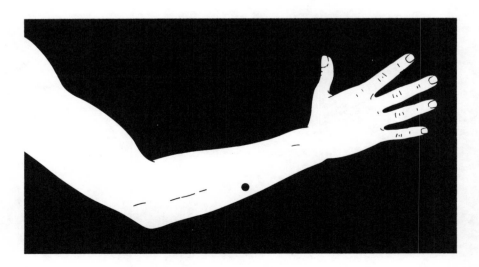

## LARGE INTESTINE # 10

This is a hit-point located between the radiobrachialis and the extensor carpi radialis longus, on a branch of the radial nerve. It is approximately one inch down from the elbow joint on the outside of the forearm. Striking this point will produce numbness in the arm, and cause an opponent's head to come forward, exposing head and neck points to follow-up attack.

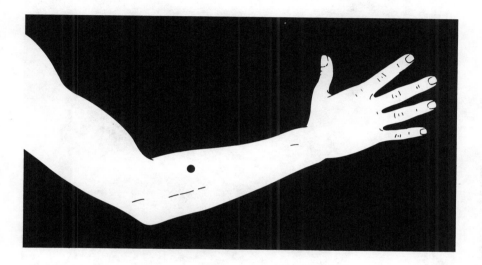

# LARGE INTESTINE # 13

This is a hit-point located two inches above the crease of the elbow in the hollow on the outside of the biceps. Attack this point in and towards the body to bend the elbow and release the hand. LI-13 responds best to a strike, but may also be pressed.

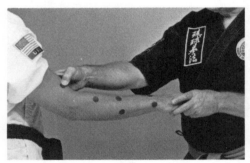

close-up

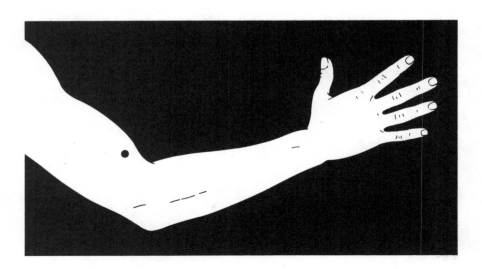

# POINTS ON THE BACK OF THE ARM

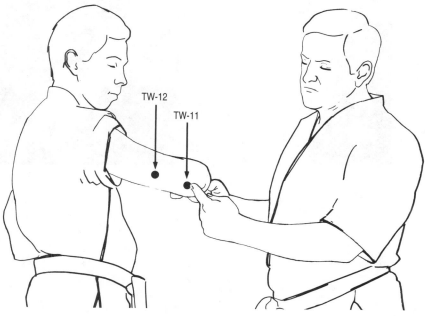

TW-12

TW-11

## TRIPLE WARMER # 11

This is a knead-point one inch above the point of the elbow. It lies over the tendon which connects the triceps to the elbow joint. At the point where a nerve connects to a tendon lies a collection of nerve cells and tendon cells which monitor the condition of the joint. This nerve/tendon cluster is called a "body of Golgi's". Stimulating this point causes the muscles of the elbow and shoulder to reflexively relax, allowing the joint to be easily locked.

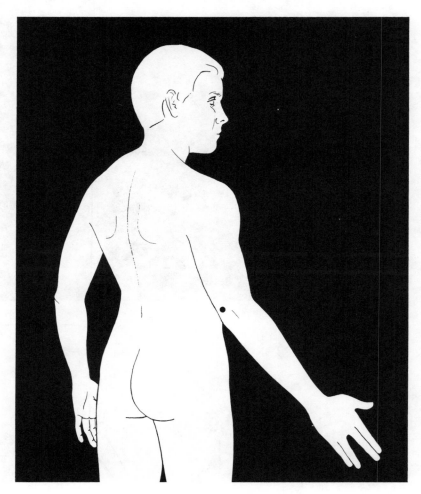

## TRIPLE WARMER # 12

This is a hit-point located directly in the middle of the triceps. A strike against this point while grasping the wrist will lock out the arm and shoulder, knocking an opponent to the ground.

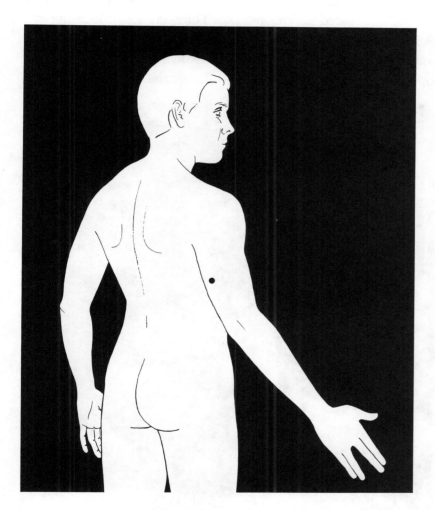

Though everyone has these pressure points, not everyone is equally susceptible on every point. Individuals with powerful forearms are resistant to blows against LI-10 and L-5. People of African descent are resistant to blows against TW-12. However, even when there is resistance to the technique applied at one of these points, it can still be used to set-up a corresponding point elsewhere. And, if any point is resistant, the next point up is usually very sensitive. For example, individuals resistant at L-5 will generally respond well to a strike against LI-13.

## ADVANCED POINTS

Pressure points on the head are obviously more dangerous, and are presented here with some reservation. Yet, we believe that serious and dedicated martial artists have the right to know and understand something of the true depth of their art. **We strongly recommend that the reader refrain from striking these points at all, and merely indicate them during practice.** In our research, we have found that it is not necessary to actually knock a training partner unconscious. A light, but well placed technique causes a blinking and unfocusing of the eyes, as well as a wobbling of the legs, which is sufficient to demonstrate for us the effectiveness of the techniques. However, we do not indiscriminately strike points on the head—we always practice with restraint.

George A. Dillman works on Dennis Rappe and answers seminar questions. The Dillman seminars have been conducted in fifteen countries and videos on this subject sold in seventeen countries.
Photo by George Owens

# POINTS OF THE HEAD AND NECK

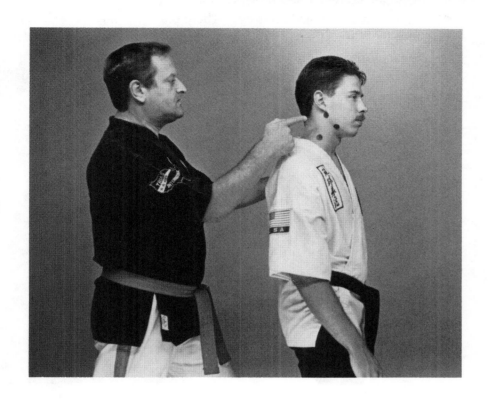

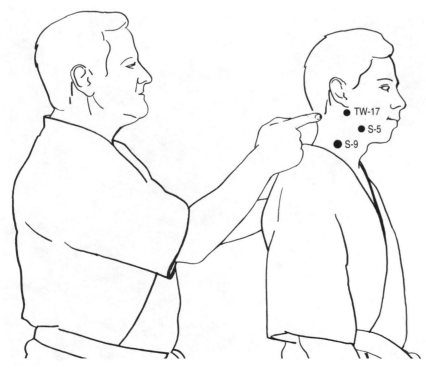

## STOMACH # 5

The stomach meridian has two descending branches on the face, one from the temple area, and the other from under the eye. These branches intersect at S-5, which is located at the notch along the bottom of the jaw bone. Through this notch passes the facial artery; and over it lies the Marginal Mandibular Branch of the Seventh Cranial (or Facial) nerve. This point is struck diagonally upward, towards the center of the skull.

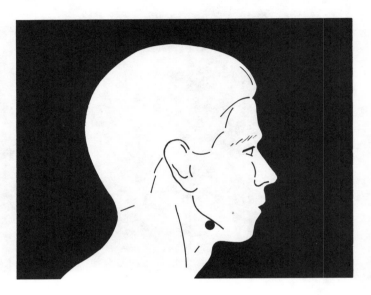

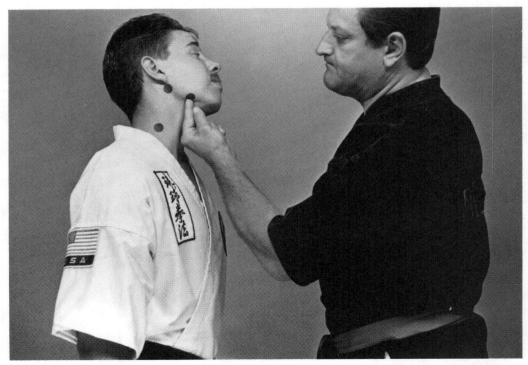

## STOMACH # 9

S-9 lies on the side of the neck at the meeting of the anterior border of the Sternocleidomastoid muscle and the thyroid cartilage. It is level with the Adam's apple in the crease between the larynx and the muscle. This point is struck at a 45° angle, with a "heavy" (not snapping) blow.

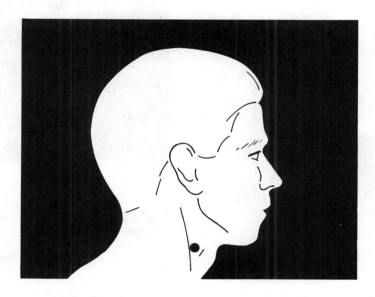

## TRIPLE WARMER # 17

TW-17 is located under the ear, behind the hinge of the jaw, at the place where the Seventh Cranial (or Facial) nerve surfaces. This point is struck at a 45° angle from back to front.

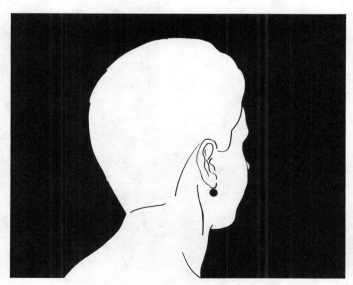

# LEARNING POINTS

The process of learning pressure points begins by becoming familiar with them. The following exercises are not combat techniques (though some of them could be if the intensity were turned up). Rather, these are exercises designed to acquaint the student with pressure points.

**Left:** Greg Dillon, demonstrates the "Pressure Points" to attack with the augmented block from kata.

## EXERCISE # 1

(1) Have a training partner hold a strong fist. With one hand, grasp your partner's arm (being careful not to be on pressure points), and place the other hand on the back of your partner's fist.  Have your partner resist while you try to force the wrist to bend.

(2) Then, grasp your partner's fist with both hands, so that your thumbs are on the back of the fist, and your little fingers press on wrist points H-6 and L-8.

(3) As your partner resists, knead your fingers into the pressure points while trying to bend the wrist.  Your partner should feel his fist becoming weak after just a few seconds, and the wrist will bend easily.

## EXERCISE # 2

(1) Have your partner form a fist, and with the side of one finger strike downward on L-7.
(2) Your partner should experience an electric tingle shooting through the thumb and index finger.

**Note:** *you may do this exercise on yourself.*

## EXERCISE # 3

(1) Have your partner form a fist and strike against L-6 (using the foreknuckles, as though knocking on a door), in the direction of the fist.
(2) Your partner should experience pain at the pressure point and a weakening of the fist.

## EXERCISE # 4

(1 & 2) Strike your partner's arm at LI-10. He should experience pain and a numbing sensation of the arm.

## EXERCISE # 5

(1) Support your partner's forearm at the wrist with one hand, and strike L-5 down and toward the fist.
(2) With a moderate blow, your partner's head should come forward slightly, and after a split-second delay his knees should buckle.

## EXERCISE # 6

This exercise is good for indicating how points work together.  Have your partner hold his arm  out.

(1) With two fingers strike H-2.  Your partner should experience a tingling sensation.

(2) Next, with one hand, grasp your partner's wrist, applying pressure on H-6 and L-8, and again strike or press H-2 with two fingers.  This time, your partner should experience the electric tingle all the way to his little finger.

## EXERCISE # 7

(1) Have your partner hold out an arm, slightly bent.  Grasp the wrist with one hand,  and have your partner resist as you strike on TW-11, as if to force an arm bar (***be careful***).  Your partner should have no trouble resisting.

(2) Next, have your partner resist as you knead your foreknuckles, moving them in a vibrating motion towards and away from the shoulder, on TW-11.

continued

## EXERCISE # 7

*continued from previous page*

(3 & 4) Pull back to your hip with your right hand while continuing the vibrating motion with your left. You should be able to easily straighten your partner's arm and lock the elbow.

## EXERCISE # 8

(1) Have your partner hold his arm as in the previous exercise. This time, grasp the wrist with one hand and push against TW-12 with your other hand as you attempt to straighten the arm. Your partner should have no trouble resisting.
(2 & 3) Next, strike TW-12 with the bony prominence of your wrist. This time you will be able to easily straighten the arm and lock the elbow.

***Caution:*** *do not strike too hard.*

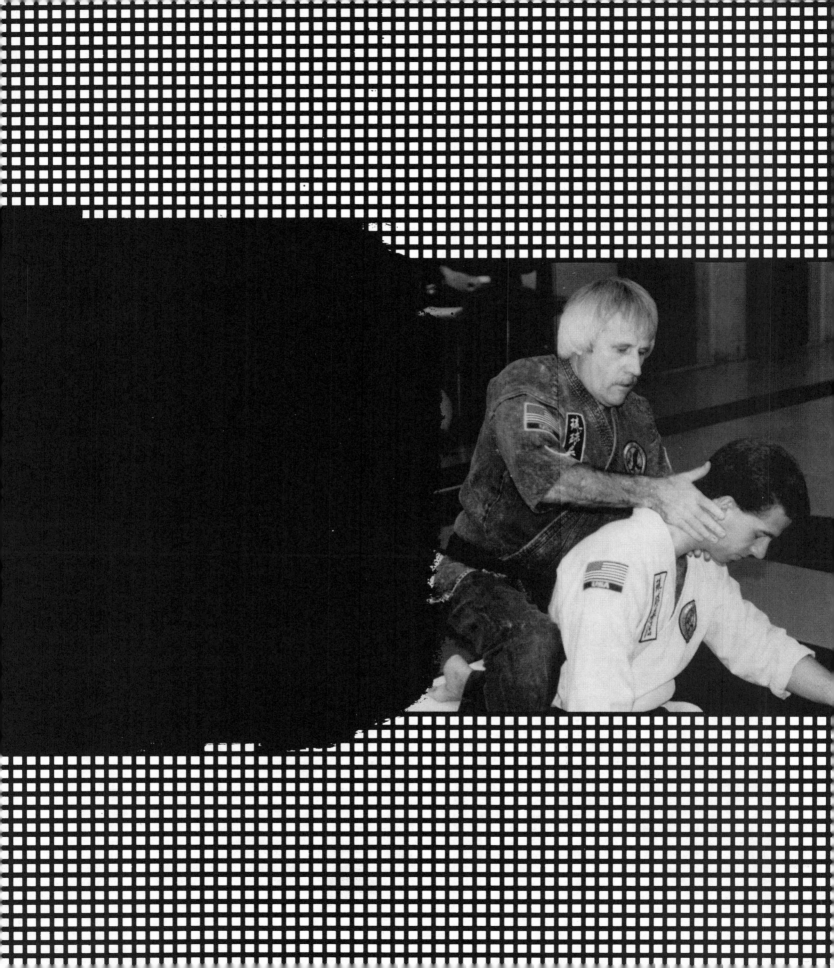

# ENERGY RESTORATION

Generally speaking, the immediate results of a strike to a pressure point (for example, the numbing of the arm caused by striking LI-10) lasts twenty minutes. The total effect on the disrupted energy flow, however, takes about 72 hours to resolve itself. Therefore, it is important to take steps to restore the proper current of energy in order to minimize any lingering effects of a training session.

## ARM RESUSCITATION

When striking a pressure point, force must be sharply focused. This is done by using some small hard part of the body such as a single knuckle, or the bony prominence of the wrist. When we consider that an acupuncturist uses very tiny needles to manipulate energy flow, it is easy to understand how a serious and focused blow can cause such a profound and instantaneous effect on the body.

**Left:** Bob Golden, does revival to bring back opponent's full energy.
Photo by Jim Duncan.

The peculiar thing about energy restoration is that it is done the same way as the attack.  The basic rule is: Hit to disrupt energy, hit again to restore it.  The strike to restore is performed on the same point as the most powerful hit.  For example, if while grasping L-8 with one hand, you punch LI-10, the restoration is applied to LI-10.  The restoration, though,  is different from the attack in two ways: first, only half as much force is exerted (hit only half as hard); second, where the attack is done with a hard knobby surface, the healing is performed with the palm of the hand (a firm slap).

After the healing slap, it is important to massage the area to stimulate the flow of energy through the meridians.  Because each meridian has a particular direction of flow—either towards the body or away from it—massage in the direction of energy flow.

The meridians on the inner aspect of the arm have an energy flow from the body towards the hand.  Energy in the meridians on the outer aspect of the arm flows from the hands towards the body.  However, when in doubt, massage in a circle.

## MERIDIANS OF THE ARM

HEART: Flows away from the body and ends at the tip of the little finger.

SMALL INTESTINE: Begins at the tip of the little finger and flows towards the body.

PERICARDIUM: (Also called Heart Constrictor, or Circulation/Sex) Flows from the body and ends at the tip of the middle finger.

TRIPLE WARMER: Begins at the tip of the ring finger and flows towards the body.

LUNG: Flows from the body and ends at the tip of the thumb. (DIAGRAMS 30 & 31)

LARGE INTESTINE:Begins at the tip of the index finger and flows towards the body.

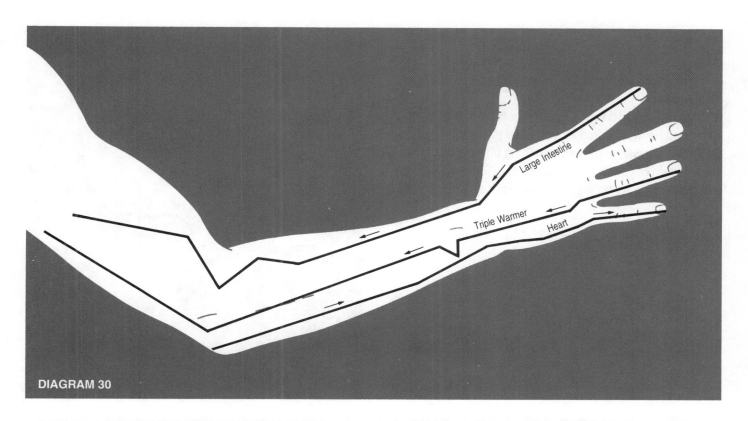

DIAGRAM 30

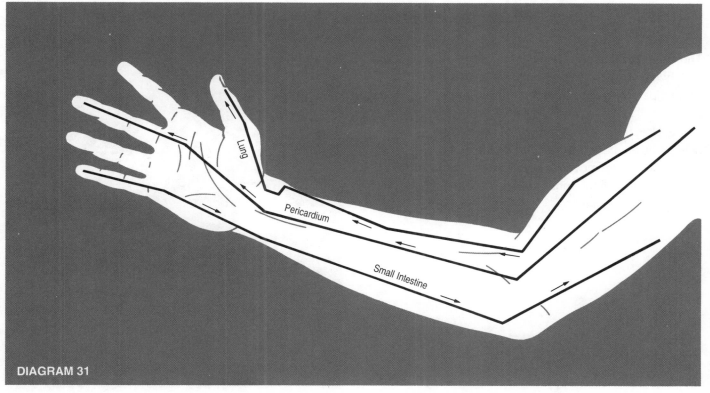

DIAGRAM 31

## METHOD # 1

(1) To practice the basic restoration technique, begin by striking your partner on LI-10 to produce pain and numbness.

(2) Then, slap LI-10 with a cupped palm using about half as much force as you used in the hit.

(3) Firmly rub with your palm, pushing upward in the direction of your partner's shoulder. The slap and massage may be repeated as necessary.

## METHOD # 2

This next technique is a general method of restoring energy to the body. It may be used when a person is conscious, but feeling weak or faint.

(1 & 2) Hold your partner's hand between both palms, rub vigorously—the hand on the outer aspect of the arm moves towards the fingers, while the hand on the inner aspect moves towards the shoulder.

## METHOD # 3

Because the acupuncture meridians begin or end in the finger tips, the fingers are considered vital for proper energy flow. It was for this reason that the oriental practice of cutting off the little finger evolved as a form of discipline. By removing the little finger, the Heart meridian was impeded. This was believed to reduce the tendency to aggression and non-conformity which had produced the offending behavior.

By manipulating the tips of the finger, the total restoration of energy is promoted.

(1) The method is to grasp your partner's finger with one hand, firmly supporting the first joint.

(2) Then, with the other hand, grasp the tip of the finger between your thumb and index finger.

(3) Pull the tip of the finger straight, as if to stretch it out. The finger-tip should slip out of your grasp (you are not trying to remove it), but you should also hear a faint sucking sound as the knuckle releases ever so slightly. This release of the joint opens the pathway for the flow of ki. Begin this therapy with the little finger and work up to the thumb, then repeat with the other hand. Remember also, your partner should not experience discomfort as you perform this restoration. Use this method in conjunction with the second restoration described above.

## HEAD RESUSCITATION

Head resuscitation is used to revive someone who has been stunned or knocked-out. Like arm resuscitation, it is done by striking; however, unlike the arm method, the slap is performed on the opposite side of the head from which the knock-out technique was applied.

(A) Head revival uses the "wake-up" nerve (or Spinal Accessory nerve) which runs down the hollow of the neck, on either side of the spine. This is the place that people naturally massage when they have a headache, or are tired. It is also the spot where boxing corner-men apply the ice-pack to their fighter.

## METHOD

(1) Have a training partner sit, or lie on the floor as though knocked-out or dazed (***Do not knock-out your training partner to see if you can revive him!*** ).  Sit him upright, and  help support and straighten his back with your knee (***Do not place your knee directly on the spine***).

(2) Have an assistant cross your partner's legs.

(3) With one hand, support your partner's head by cupping the chin.

(4 & 5) With the other hand, slap the "wake-up" nerve, then massage.

2

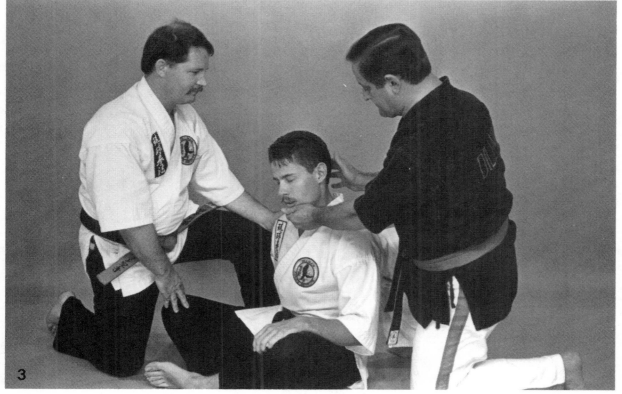

3

continued

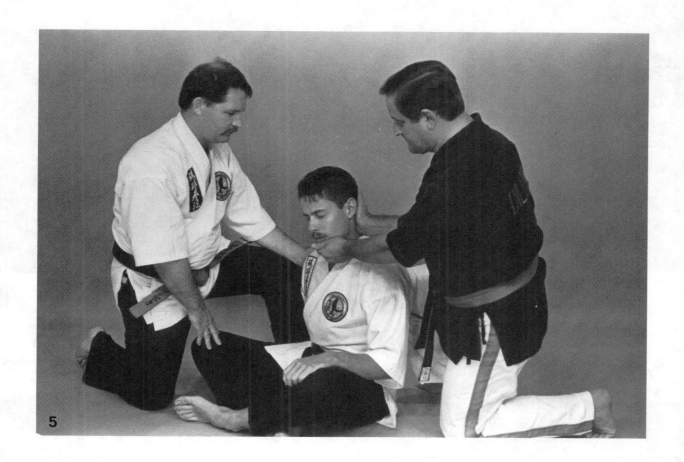

5

## IMPORTANT POINTS:

1. Strike the "wake-up" nerve on the side opposite the side struck for the knock-out. If someone is knocked out with a blow to the left side, you should strike the right side for revival. 2. Never perform the head resuscitation unless you are firmly supporting the person's head.

One final note: practitioners of all kinds of hand-healing methods—from shiatsu to touch therapy—recognize that one develops the right "touch" only with practice. This "touch", we believe, is the manifestation of ki (chi). Through practice, the healer learns to control and project the ki through the hands; therefore, do not expect to be an instant master of healing. While you should experience good initial success, it will take time to become truly adept.

"It is not my intention to make you a hand healer, but you should know how to correct points after hitting them."

*George Dillman*

# TECHNIQUES OF KYUSHO-JITSU

We have stated that the principles and techniques of pressure point fighting are contained within the kata of traditional karate. Therefore, to introduce these methods we will demonstrate applications for familiar kata movements. We will also contrast the Ryukyu kempo interpretation with explanations commonly given in karate-do training.

Because this is a beginning text on the subject, we will be specific only with respect to the pressure points already described. Certain techniques demonstrated will include attacks to body or leg points, and the reader interested in learning the location of these points will need to seek further instruction. (It is our intention to include some of this advanced material in subsequent volumes.)

Also, the reader should find that these movements can be practiced as self-defense routines, even if the source kata is unfamiliar.

In kata practice, there are several actions called "blocks". This is unfortunate because these movements do not function well as blocks at all. This is not to say that these are ineffective techniques; to the contrary, the reader will see that these so-called "blocks" produce unconsciousness and/or broken bones. The problem is one of language.

Because something is <u>called</u> a block, we assume that it <u>is</u> a block. We do not understand that in a society influenced by the philosophies of Buddhism and Taoism, a name is merely a label given for convenience sake. A thing is not what its name implies, because its reality cannot be reduced to a name. We would have been more fortunate had karate techniques been named like Chinese techniques are named. If the knife hand block had been called "Purple Dragon Sticks Out Its Tongue", perhaps we would have noticed much sooner that it is not a block at all.

To illustrate this point, we will begin with examples of "blocks" — and the "opening salutation" as well — and provide multiple applications for each.

**Left:** Ron Richards (left) knocks out Keith Huyett with a fist tap to Lung point #1. Richards has been studying the Dillman Theory from the beginning and now teaches his own seminars on this subject.

# TECHNIQUE # 1

This action is the common first move of many kata.

(1) Begin with your feet together.
(2 & 3) Raise your open left hand to chin level and place your right fist against your left palm.
(4 & 5) Draw your hands inward as you lower them in front of your body.
(6) Complete the movement as your hands reach belt level.

*In popular karate this is regarded as a "salutation". The actions of the hands are sometimes said to represent the strength of karate (fist) and the restraint of karate's ethical principles (open hand). In Ryukyu kempo, this is the first move of the kata, and therefore has combat applications.*

2

3

5

6

## APPLICATION # 1

**PRESSURE POINTS: DIAGRAM 32**

(1) Your opponent threatens you by shaking his right fist at you (represented by your right fist in the kata movement).

(2) You grasp your opponent's wrist with your left hand, pressing on points L-7 and SI-6.

(3) With your right hand press on the back of your opponent's fist at TW-3 (in the kata, your left hand touches the back of your right fist at TW-3) bending his wrist over.

(4) Press your opponent's bent wrist downward towards the floor (exactly as in the kata).

1

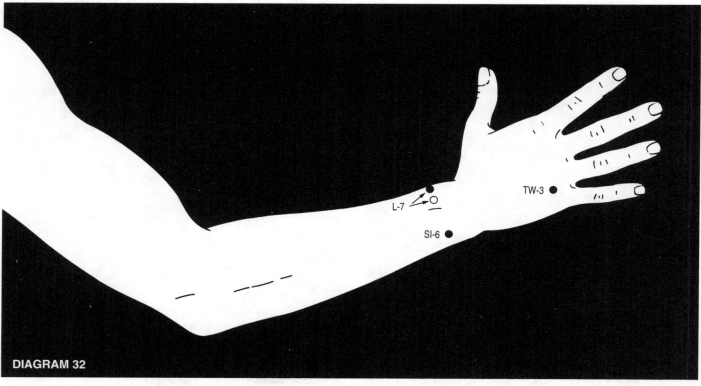

DIAGRAM 32

## APPLICATION # 2

### PRESSURE POINTS: DIAGRAM 33

(1) Your opponent threatens you with his right fist.
(2) Catch his fist with your left hand and draw it towards you.
(3) Strike forcefully with your right fist against TW-3 (as in the kata, the right fist into left palm). If you break the fourth metacarpal bone at the location TW-3, your opponent will be rendered helpless.

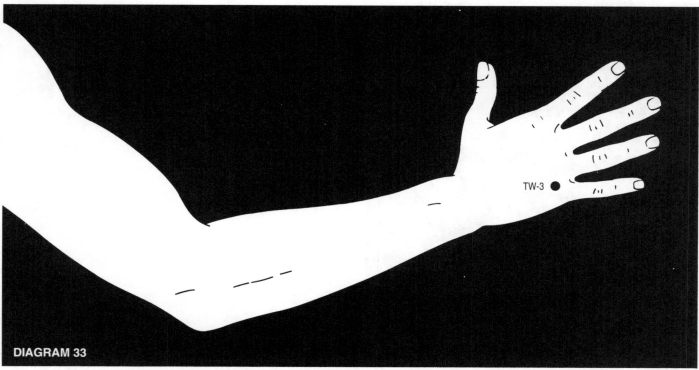

DIAGRAM 33

## APPLICATION # 3

**PRESSURE POINTS: DIAGRAM 34**

(1) Your opponent cocks his right hand back to punch you.

(2) Reach up with your left hand and catch him behind the neck.

(3) Pull him forward to unbalance him and stop his attack.

(4) As you pull your opponent forward, strike upward with your right fist under his jaw into S-5.

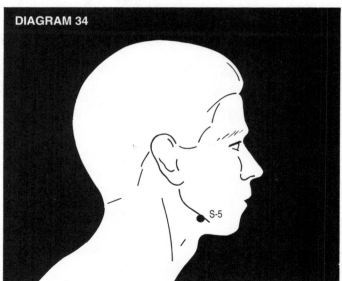

DIAGRAM 34

S-5

## TECHNIQUE # 2

This action is commonly called "downward block" and is found in virtually every kata.

(1) Extend your right arm out at stomach level and raise your left arm up so that the fist is near your right ear. This is the "set" position for a left downward block.
(2) Draw your right hand towards your hip as you sweep your left hand downward.
(3) Bring your right hand to your hip, and stop your left hand over your left leg. This final posture is considered to be the "block".

*(A) In popular karate, this action is used to block against a kick. However, this application employs the small, weak ulnar bone of the forearm against the kicking leg—an invitation to a broken arm. Further, the action exposes the head to counter attack and is completely impractical against kicks below groin level. Finally, the movement of set and block is simply too slow for actual use in this fashion. Ryukyu kempo does not interpret this as a block at all.*

1

# APPLICATION # 1

**PRESSURE POINTS: DIAGRAM 35A & 35B**

(1) Your opponent seizes your right wrist with his left hand.

(2) Reach your right hand around his left hand and grasp his wrist on SI-6.

(3) Turn your right palm downward, turning your opponent's arm as well, and pull towards your right hip.

(4) With your left arm, execute the "downward block", striking your opponent in the middle of the triceps on TW-12.

(5) Follow through with the technique to drive your opponent downward.

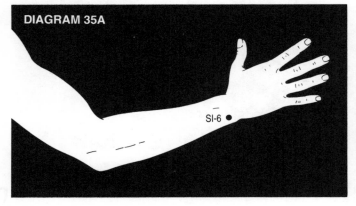

DIAGRAM 35A

SI-6

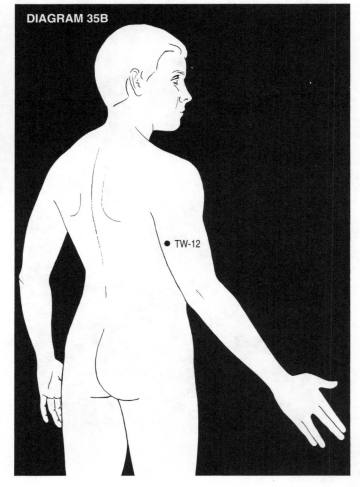

DIAGRAM 35B

TW-12

# APPLICATION # 2

### PRESSURE POINTS: DIAGRAM 36A & 36B

(1) Your opponent grabs your right wrist with his right hand.

(2) Bring your right hand up inside to rotate his arm.

(3) Reach around and grab his wrist on points SI-6 and L-7.

(4) Place the foreknuckles of your left hand against TW-11, just above your opponent's elbow.

(5 & 6) Twist and draw your right fist to your hip as you knead TW-11, driving your opponent to the floor.

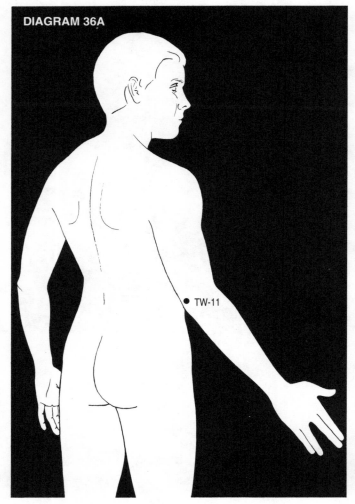

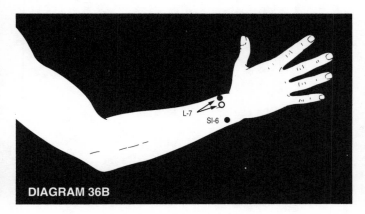

DIAGRAM 36A

TW-11

L-7

SI-6

DIAGRAM 36B

## APPLICATION # 3

(1) Your opponent grabs your lapel with his left hand.

(2) Grasp his elbow with your left hand.

(3) Reach up with your right hand and grab his hair on the back of his head near his right ear. This corresponds to the set position of the downward block.

(4) Pull his left elbow to your left hip, while pulling his head down and around.

(5) Complete the technique pulling your opponent down onto your front knee.

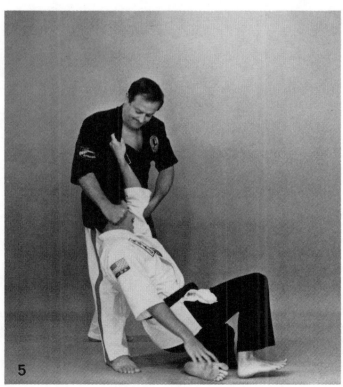

## TECHNIQUE # 3

This common kata movement is called a "side block", or "middle block".

1) Bring your right fist up at about chin level, and place your left fist near your right elbow. This is the "set" position.
(2) Draw your right fist towards your hip and sweep your left fist out and towards the left.
(3) Bring your right fist to your hip and your left fist even with the left shoulder, the elbow bent about 90°.  This is the completed "block".

*(A) In popular karate this technique is explained as a defense against a punch. Unfortunately, this movement is far too slow to be used in an actual fight as it is practiced. Ryukyu kempo applications, however, allow the complete action to be used effectively.*

1

## APPLICATION # 1

### PRESSURE POINTS: DIAGRAM 37A & 37B

(1) Your opponent grabs your lapel with his left hand and threatens you with his right fist.

(2 & 3) With your right hand grasp your opponent's wrist at points H-6 and L-8.

(4 & 5) Strike the top of the forearm near the elbow at L-5 with your left fist. This corresponds to the "set" position in the kata movement. This causes your opponent's head to turn and drop forward.

(6) Pull your opponent's left hand towards your hip and hit the exposed side of his head as it turns, striking under the jaw at S-5, or behind the jaw at TW-17 with your left fist.

This corresponds to the completion of the kata movement.

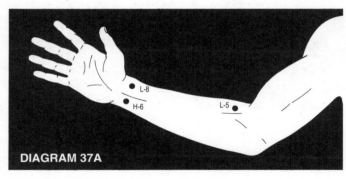

DIAGRAM 37A

DIAGRAM 37B

# APPLICATION # 2

### PRESSURE POINTS: DIAGRAM 38A & 38B

(1) Your opponent grabs your lapel with his left hand and threatens you with his right fist.

(2 & 3) With your left hand strike down on the forearm near the elbow hitting L-5, while striking across against the hinge of the jaw at TW-17 with your right fist. This is represented in the kata by the "set" position.

(4) Grasp your opponent's left wrist on pressure points H-6 & L-8 with your right hand.

(5) Pull his left hand towards your right hip and strike S-9 on the side of the neck with your left hand. This is the completed "block".

1

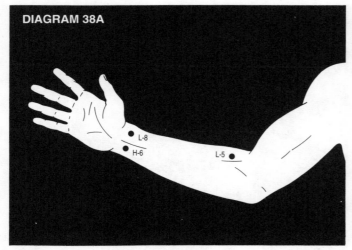

DIAGRAM 38A

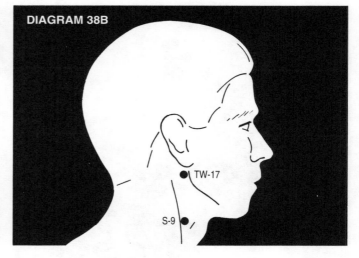

DIAGRAM 38B

## APPLICATION # 3

### PRESSURE POINTS: DIAGRAM 39A & 39B

(1) Your opponent grabs your lapel with his left hand and threatens you with his right fist.

(2) With your right hand grasp your opponent's wrist at points H-6 and L-8.

(3) Taking the placement of your left fist near the right elbow in the "set" position of the kata movement as an indicator, punch the inside of your opponent's arm just above the elbow at H-2 with your left hand.

(4) The side of your opponent's neck moves to the side exposing S-9 as you follow through against H-2.

(5) Strike S-9 point with your left fist, (or the bony prominence of your wrist,) while maintaining a grip on the wrist points with your right hand.

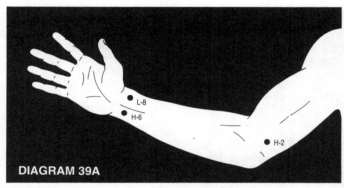

DIAGRAM 39A

DIAGRAM 39B

# TECHNIQUE # 4

The "knife hand" block is another common movement of kata. There are two different methods of performance, with various styles favoring one over the other.

**METHOD A**

(1) Bring both the left and the right hands up to head level on the left side of the body. This is the "set" position.
(2) Swing the hands forward in unison.
(3) End with the right hand extended and the left hand resting near the abdomen.

129

continued

## TECHNIQUE # 4

*Continued from previous page*

**METHOD B**

(1) Bring the right hand up near the left ear, and extend the left hand forward. This is the "set" position.

(2) Swing the right hand forward while drawing the left hand back towards the abdomen.

(3) End with the right hand extended and the left hand resting near the abdomen.

*(A) In popular karate either method is described as blocking a punch. The extended right hand catches the incoming punch at the wrist. Unfortunately, the complete movement is too slow to actually be applied in this fashion in real combat. Further, the "knife hand block" occurs alone in kata, without any follow-up technique, implying that it can be used to disable an attacker by itself.*

1

## APPLICATION # 1

### PRESSURE POINTS: DIAGRAM 40A & 40B

(1) Your opponent prepares to attack with a wide right-handed punch.

(2) Using "Method A", bring both hands up to strike your opponent's arm, catching L-7 with your left hand, and L-6 with your right. (Note that this movement employs the "set" position not merely to block, but to activate pressure points).

(3 & 4) Counterstrike by chopping against S-9 with the right hand.

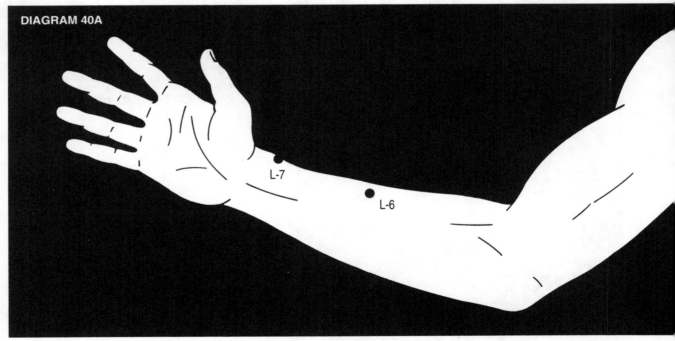

DIAGRAM 40A

L-7

L-6

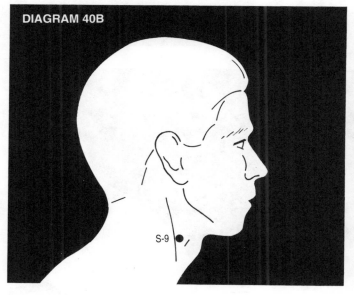

**DIAGRAM 40B**

S-9

## APPLICATION # 2

### PRESSURE POINTS: DIAGRAM 41A, 41B & 41C

(1) Your opponent prepares to attack with a wide right-handed punch.

(2) As your opponent swings, use "Method B", strike L-6 on his forearm with your right hand, while spearing his body with your left hand.

(3) Grasp your opponent's arm firmly with your left hand, pressing your thumb into the side of the biceps at LI-13, and your fingers on the inside of the arm at H-2, while striking the side of his neck at S-9.

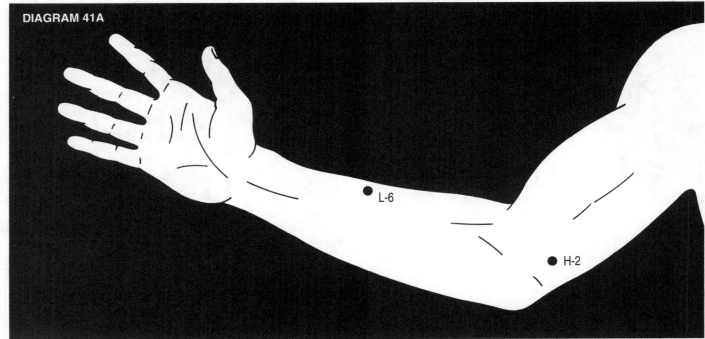

DIAGRAM 41A

L-6

H-2

2

3

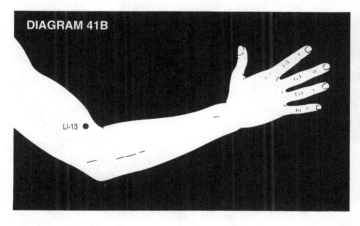

DIAGRAM 41B

LI-13

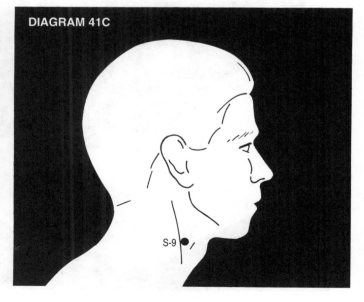

DIAGRAM 41C

S-9

# APPLICATION # 3

### PRESSURE POINTS: DIAGRAM 42A, 42B & 42C

(1) Your opponent grabs your lapel with his right hand and threatens you with his left fist.
(2) With your left hand grasp your opponent's arm just above the elbow, pressing LI-13 with your thumb, and H-2 with your fingers.
(3) Reach your right hand forward defensively.

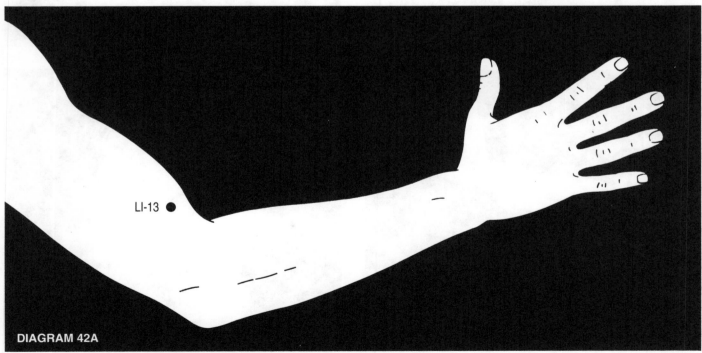

DIAGRAM 42A

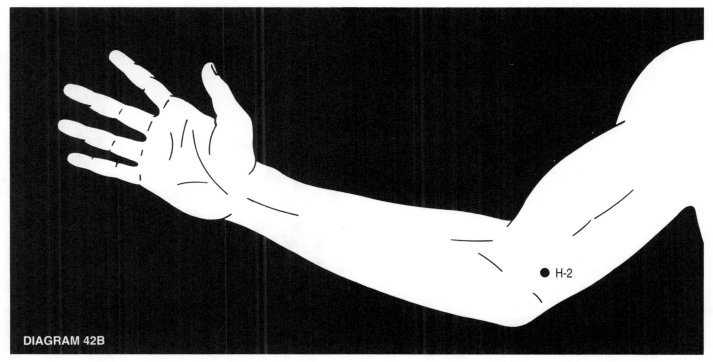

DIAGRAM 42B

● H-2

continued

# APPLICATION # 3

*Continued from previous page*

(4) Use the knuckle of your right thumb (Diagram 43) to strike TW-17 at the hinge of the jaw, on the left side of his face.

(5) Follow through with your right hand, bringing it back to your left ear to assume the "set" position.

(6) Continuing to hold your opponent firmly with your left hand, strike him again, this time using a right chop to the side of his neck at S-9.

**Warning: this technique crosses the head, striking vital points on both sides. Do not hit these points in practice.**

4

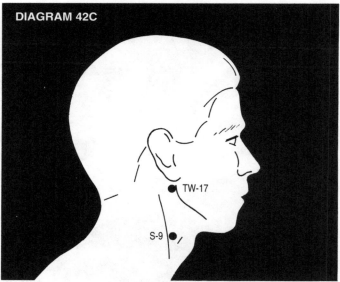

DIAGRAM 42C

TW-17

S-9

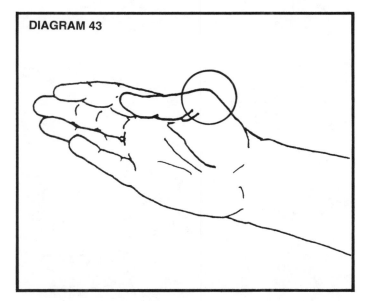

**DIAGRAM 43**

## TECHNIQUE # 5

The "upward", or "rising" block is found in several kata, especially the basic kata such as the Taikyoku and Pinan (Heian) series.

(1) Bring your right arm across your body at belt level, and extend your left hand slightly forward. This is the "set" position.

(2) Draw your right arm upward and slightly to the right in a sweeping motion, while drawing your left hand back towards your hip.

(3) Complete the movement with your palm turned outward, even with the top of your head and your left fist at your hip. This is the complete "block".

*(A) In popular karate, this is explained as a block against an attack to the head. Unfortunately, it is once again too slow for use in actual combat. It also uses the small bone of the forearm, the ulna, as the blocking surface.*

*(B) Further, raising the arm over the head to block completely opens the chest, exposing numerous vital points to attack. The Ryukyu kempo applications do not have this fault, because the opponent is completely helpless by the time the arm is raised to head height.*

1

A

# APPLICATION # 1

**PRESSURE POINTS: DIAGRAM 44A & 44B**

(1) Your opponent reaches to grab you with his right hand.

(2) Catch his hand at the wrist with your left hand, grasping on L-8 and H-6.

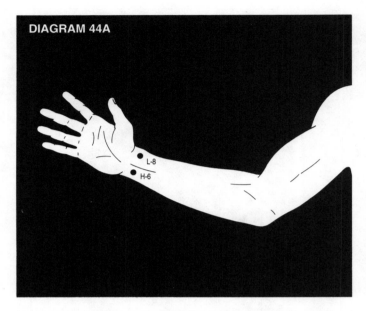

DIAGRAM 44A

L-8

H-6

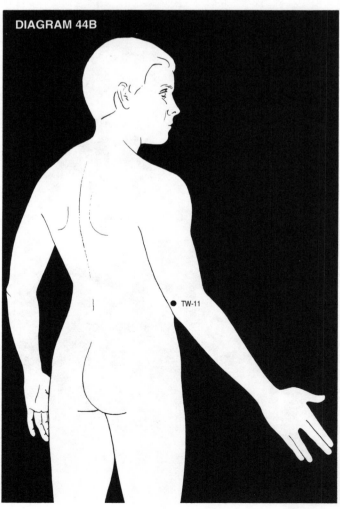

DIAGRAM 44B

TW-11

continued

## APPLICATION # 1

*Continued from previous page*

(3) Twist his arm, palm up, and pull it toward your left hip.

(4) Bring your right arm underneath his captured right arm and press upward just above the elbow at TW-11 with the thumb side of your wrist.

(5) Roll your wrist against TW-11 to stimulate the body of Golgi's nerve point.

(6) As the shoulder and elbow release, raise upward and to the right with your right arm, while pulling downward with your left to break your opponent's elbow. (Remember to use restraint if practicing these moves!)

## APPLICATION # 2

### PRESSURE POINTS: DIAGRAM 45A & 45B

(1) Your opponent punches towards your stomach with his right fist.

(2) With your left hand, catch your opponent's right wrist, pressing on H-6 and L-8, and pull it towards your left hip.

(3 & 4) Strike down with your right arm against L-5 near the crease of his elbow.

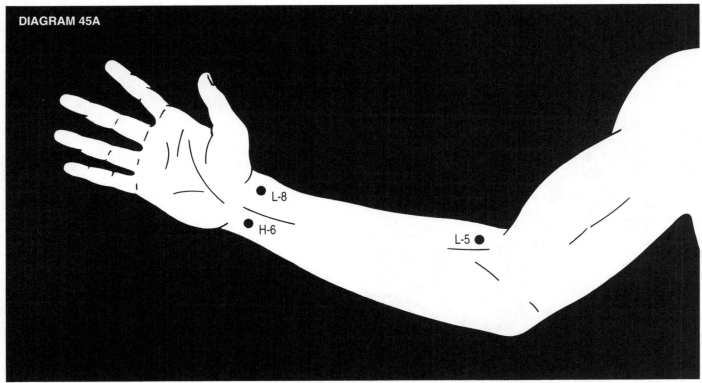

DIAGRAM 45A

L-8

H-6

L-5

continued

## APPLICATION # 2

*Continued from previous page*

(5, 6 & 7) As his knees buckle and his head comes forward strike upwards with your right arm, hitting S-5 in the middle of your opponent's jaw with your forearm.

**Caution: The strike to L-5 will bring the opponent's head forward very quickly, so control is difficult in training.**

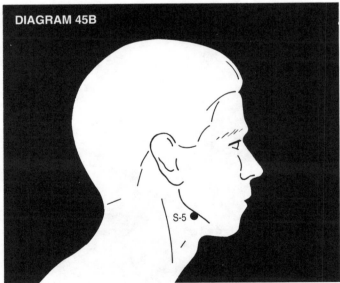

DIAGRAM 45B

S-5

# SPECIFIC KATA TECHNIQUES

In this next section we will look at techniques and sequences from specific kata. As we contrast the common karate-do interpretation with the Ryukyu kempo application it will become apparent that kata is entirely effective for real combat. It will also become apparent just how little kata has been understood in western practice.

We do realize that any particular school of karate-do may teach a better explanation for a given movement than the "karate" explanation we show. However, each karate interpretation given is consistent with what has been taught or demonstrated in a large number of schools and books. Furthermore, while a specific school may teach a good application for one particular kata movement, it generally does not provide consistently excellent meanings for the entire kata. By contrast, in Ryukyu kempo we teach only truly effective applications, or none at all. If we do not have a real application for a movement we simply admit that we do not yet understand its meaning.

We will only show one Ryukyu kempo application for each sequence so that we can touch on several different kata from several different systems. However, as we have already illustrated, each sequence has more than one effective application.

**Left:** George A. Dillman knocks out Rick Clark in the Midwest USA.

## PINAN SHODAN

The Pinan (Heian, in Japanese) kata series was developed by Anko (Yositsune) Itosu in 1907. These five kata were created for teaching school children. Nonetheless, they contain many effective pressure point techniques. The following is the opening sequence of Pinan shodan (Pinan 1), though in some styles the order of Pinan shodan and nidan is reversed and this kata is called Pinan 2.

(1) Begin standing in a shoulder-width natural stance (shizen-tai) with your fists extended in front of you.
(2) Turn to the left and assume a left cat stance, bringing your right arm up to your head, and your left arm out as in a "side block".
(3 & 4) Bring your left fist back towards your right shoulder as you sweep your right fist forward.
(5) Draw your right fist to your hip as you punch with your left hand.

## KARATE-DO APPLICATION

(1) Stand facing forward as an opponent threatens you from the left.

(2) As your opponent attacks with a right punch to your face, turn and assume a cat-stance, raising both arms up but blocking only with your left.

(3) As your opponent presses the attack with a left punch, deflect the attack with your left arm while striking his elbow with your right fist.

(4) Counter with your own left punch before the opponent can continue the attack.

*The main problem with this application is that it allows the opponent's first attack to go unanswered, and assumes the second punch will be aimed at the head for the trapping strike against his elbow, even though the side of the body is completely exposed. It also leaves one hand idle during the first and fourth steps.*

## RYUKYU KEMPO APPLICATION

### PRESSURE POINTS: DIAGRAM 46A, 46B & 46C

(1) An assailant threatens you with a right punch. Face him directly.

(2) As your opponent punches at your head, angle your body sideways, while assuming a cat stance, and catch his punch (see appendix "A") with your left hand, grasping on the wrist pressure points (L-7, SI-6).

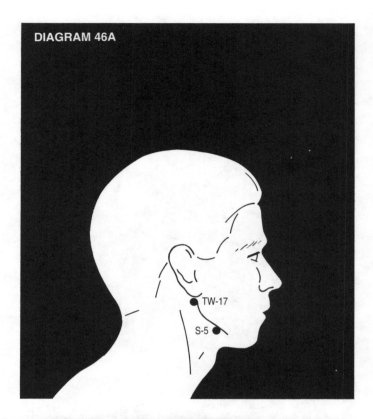

DIAGRAM 46A

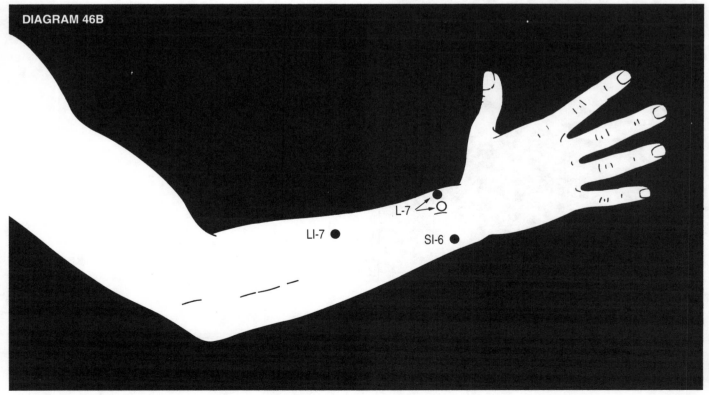

DIAGRAM 46B

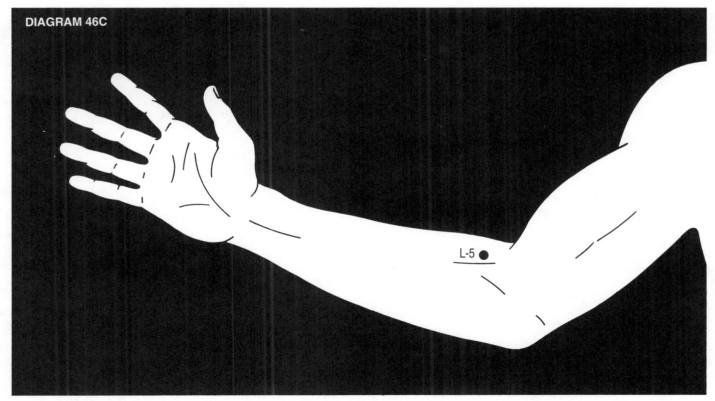

DIAGRAM 46C

L-5 ●

continued

# RYUKYU KEMPO APPLICATION

*Continued from previous page*

(3) Pull his arm, stretching him off balance while you strike under the ear at TW-17 with your right foreknuckles.

(4, 5 & 6) Skip step two of the kata movement, and go directly to step three, striking the other side of your opponent's head under the jaw at S-5, while pulling his left arm down to your hip.

**Note:** *This technique may be performed on either side regardless of which hand the opponent uses.*

**Warning: as shown, this technique crosses the head striking vital points on both sides. Do not hit these points in practice!**

continued

## RYUKYU KEMPO APPLICATION
*Continued from previous page*

(7 & 8) If instead of punching, the opponent seizes your lapel with his right hand, assume a cat stance, but otherwise skip the first step of the kata sequence.

(9 & 10) Strike forward and down with your right fist near the opponent's elbow on L-5, while striking back towards your right shoulder with your left fist, hitting the middle of his forearm at LI-7. (Perform this action exactly as in the kata to hit the points at the correct angles.)

(11) The strike to the points will cause your opponent's knees to buckle, and his head will turn as it comes forward, exposing the side of his face.

(12) Punch under his right ear at TW-17 with your right fist.

7

10

8

9

11

12

## PINAN SANDAN

(1) Begin standing upright with your fist on your hips, your elbows to the sides.
(2) Step forward with your right leg into a side horse stance.
(3) Swing your right elbow forward, past the line of your body.
(4) Recover your right elbow, bringing it back in line with your hips.
(5 & 6) Perform a backfist strike with your right hand.

## KARATE-DO APPLICATION

(1, 2 & 3) As your opponent attacks with a right punch, step forward into a side horse stance and block with your elbow.

(4) Immediately counter with a right backfist strike.

*The weakness of this application is the basic premise that any person would block with his hands on his hips. If the defender's hands are trapped, wouldn't the attacker aim for the undefended face? Also, the basic timing — punch, counter — puts the defender's counter in a race with the attacker's follow-up move.*

# RYUKYU KEMPO APPLICATION

**PRESSURE POINTS: DIAGRAM 48A ,48B & 48C**

(1)  Your opponent grabs your right wrist with his left hand.

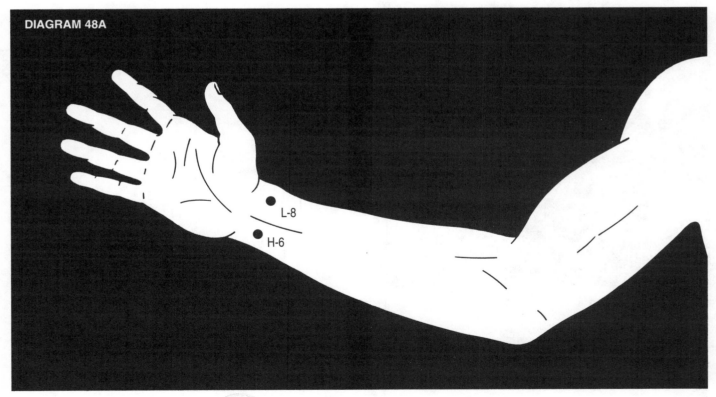

DIAGRAM 48A

L-8

H-6

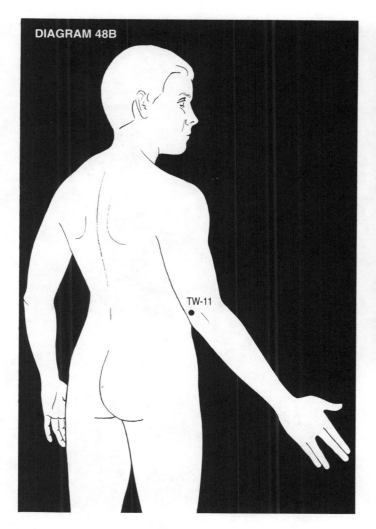

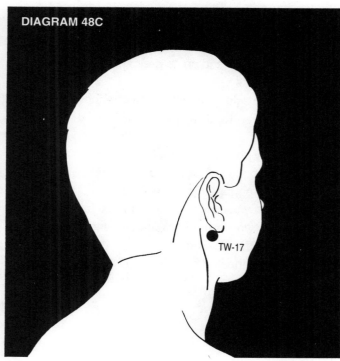

continued

## RYUKYU KEMPO APPLICATION

*Continued from previous page*

(2) Twist your right hand up, to grasp his left wrist on pressure points L-8 & H-6.

(3) Step forward with your left foot and reach your left arm over his elbow placing your fist on your own hip.

(4) The knobby portion of your elbow rests exactly on the body of Golgi's pressure point located at your opponent's elbow (TW-11). Bring your elbow back in line with your hip (as in the kata), locking your attacker's arm and causing him to double over.

(5) Strike him at the hinge of the jaw (TW-17) with your left fist.

## PINAN YONDAN

(1) Step out with the left foot on the diagonal and cross your hands in front of your stomach (in what is called a low "X-block").
(2, 3 & 4) Raise the arms up to shoulder height, then draw them apart, palms facing forward (in what is called a "reverse wedge block").

continued

## PINAN YONDAN

*Continued from previous page*

(5 & 6) Front kick with the right leg.
(7) Step forward and execute a left reverse punch.
(8) Follow immediately with a right punch.

**Note:** *some styles do not show step # 1 as a separate action, but simply as the preparation, or, "set" position, for the "reverse wedge block".*

5

## KARATE-DO APPLICATION

(1) As your opponent attacks with a front kick, reach down and block with your crossed wrists.

(2) As your opponent presses the assault with a double punch (morote-zuki), block the attack with your hands from the inside outward.

(3) Seize the initiative by launching your own kicking attack.

(4) Then continue with punches.

*This application is faulty at several points; (5) the x-block against a kick exposes the defender's head to the opponent's follow-up attack. Further, the x-block will only work if the attacker kicks high enough (at least groin level) to reach with the block.*

*The reverse wedge block is also faulty in application. As applied, it pits the defender's weakest muscles against the opponent's strongest muscles. The action of pulling the arms towards the centerline of the body (adduction) is much stronger than the action of pushing the arms away from the centerline (abduction). (6) The action of trying to force the attacker's punch outward (or worse, trying to pry apart a two-hand lapel grab, as some styles interpret this) immediately puts the defender at the disadvantage from a strictly bio-mechanical standpoint.*

*And finally, if the attacker is allowed to charge in with a kick and a punch, he will have the advantage simply in terms of momentum, and will continue to attack, running the defender over.*

# RYUKYU KEMPO APPLICATION

**PRESSURE POINTS: DIAGRAM 49A, 49B & 49C**

(1) The attacker grabs your left wrist with his right hand.

(2) With your right hand reach under his right wrist and press upward against his vital point, SI-6.

(3) As his wrist bends back, trap his hand between your wrists, drawing up and in, raising him onto his toes. His left leg is now completely vulnerable to attack.

(4 & 5) With a right front kick, strike the inside of your attacker's exposed left leg.

1

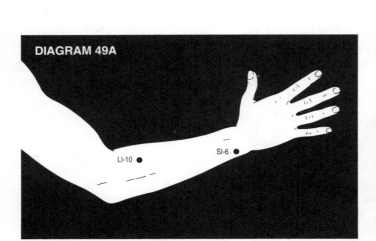

DIAGRAM 49A

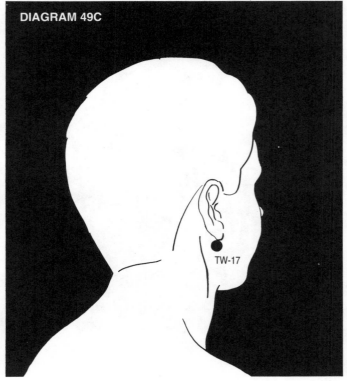

DIAGRAM 49C

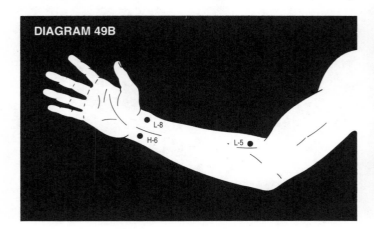

DIAGRAM 49B

continued

## RYUKYU KEMPO APPLICATION

*Continued from previous page*

(6 & 7) If, however, your opponent pulls his hand away before you are able to trap his wrist, grab his arm firmly, grasping wrist points H-6 and L-8 with your right hand, and points LI-10 and L-5 near his elbow with your left hand.

(8) Kick your opponent's left leg with a right front kick.

(9 & 10) Continue with punches to pressure point TW-17 under the ear.

## NAIHANCHI SHODAN

There are three Naihanchi kata (called Tekki among Japanese styles) which are widely practiced. Yet, these forms are often disliked by students and instructors who find them boring and pointless. Ryukyu kempo, however, teaches that the Naihanchi kata are all that is necessary to become a completely deadly fighter. The kata contain information on over 100 pressure points and countless truly effective combat techniques.

(1) Begin in a horse stance, looking to the right, and strike your left elbow against your right palm.
(2) Turn your head to the left, and stack your fists, left over right, at your right hip.
(3) Execute a left "downward block" to the left side.

1

## KARATE-DO APPLICATION

(1) Catch your opponent with your right hand, and pull him into an elbow smash.
(2) Look to the left for the next opponent, while bringing your hands to a "ready" position at your right hip.
(3) Block a second opponent's front kick with your left arm.

*There is no doubt that grabbing someone and pulling them into an elbow smash can be a very effective technique. However, this popular karate application does not consider any of the other elements of the kata movement. Why would someone stack both hands at the hips? The answer is that no one would, not in a real fight. Why would someone block a kick using the smallest bone of his forearm (the ulna)? The answer is that no one would, at least, not if he knew better.*

# RYUKYU KEMPO APPLICATION

## PRESSURE POINTS: DIAGRAM 50A & 50B

(1) Your opponent reaches to grab you with his right hand while preparing to punch with his left.
(2) Give him your left arm to grab onto.
(3) Place your right hand on his right hand, to secure it against your left arm.
(4) Roll your left elbow onto his arm, turning his arm over in the process.

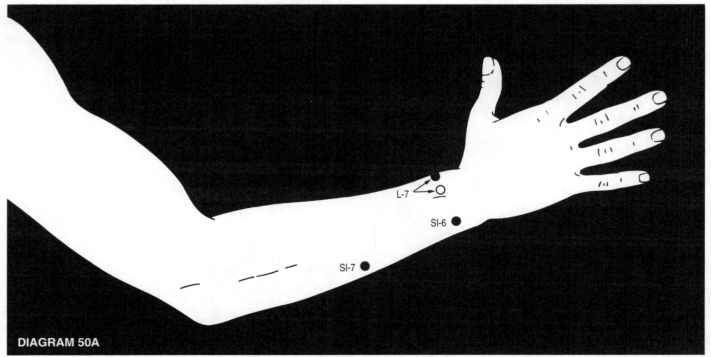

DIAGRAM 50A

2

3

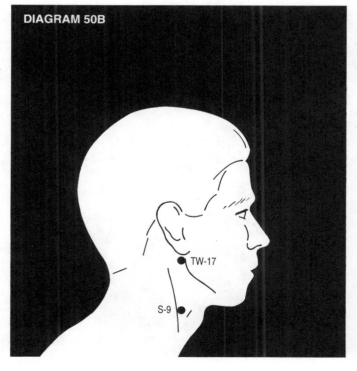

DIAGRAM 50B

TW-17

S-9

4

185

continued

## RYUKYU KEMPO APPLICATION
*Continued from previous page*

(5) Press down with your left elbow on SI-7, in the middle of his forearm along the ulnar bone.

(6 & 7) Turn towards the left and press down with your elbow to drop your opponent to the floor.

(8) With your right hand, grasp your opponent's hand, wrapping your fingers around his 5th metacarpal (little finger side of the hand) and pressing your thumb against the back of his first metacarpal (thumb side of the hand) and twist.

(9) Grasp his right wrist firmly with your left hand, at pressure points L-7 and SI-6 and pull his hand strongly to your right hip.

(10) Still holding with your right hand, strike with your left hand, either hammering the side of your opponent's neck at S-9, or (11) punching the hinge of the jaw under the ear at TW-17.

5

8

9

6

7

10

11

## WANSU KATA (A)

There are two distinct families of the kata Wansu and only the most careful examination shows that these two families grew from a common ancestor. This movement comes from a Wansu kata thought to be of a Tomari lineage.

(1) Draw both fists to the right hip, left over right, while standing upright.
(2) Execute a sidekick to the left.

## KARATE-DO APPLICATION

(1) As your opponent prepares to attack from the left, place your hands on your right hip.
(2) As he steps forward with a punch, stop him with a sidekick.

*A simple question reveals the inadequacy of this explanation: would anyone ever sidekick with both hands at one hip in a tournament or on the street?*

# RYUKYU KEMPO APPLICATION

**PRESSURE POINTS: DIAGRAM 51A & 51B**

(1) Your opponent grabs your lapel with his left hand.

(2) With your right hand grab his left fist, wrapping your fingers around the bone of his thumb (first metacarpal) and digging your thumb into TW-3 on the back of his hand between the bone of the ring and little fingers (fourth and fifth metacarpals).

(3 & 4) With your left fist, strike towards yourself against L-6 in the middle of your opponent's forearm on the thumb side.

(5) As his grip loosens, twist his hand with your right hand, as you grasp his wrist with your left hand, squeezing pressure points L-7 and SI-6.

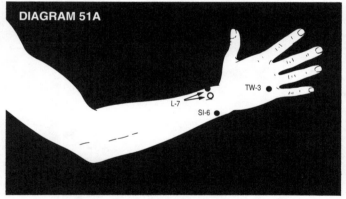

DIAGRAM 51A

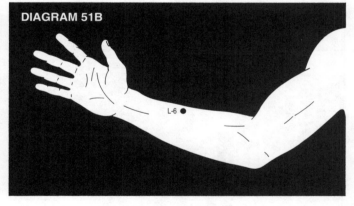

DIAGRAM 51B

continued

# RYUKYU KEMPO APPLICATION
*Continued from previous page*

(6) With a sharp twist, bring his left hand to your right hip as you turn your body sideways to him.

(7, 8, 9, 10 & 11) Attack the inside of your opponent's right leg with your left sidekick, knocking him to the floor.

6

9

## WANSU KATA (B)

This movement comes from the second family of Wansu kata, which is of Shuri lineage.

(1) Begin with your feet apart, both fists at your right hip.

(2) Step out to the left, and prepare to perform a right "downward block".

(3) Drop into a kneeling position, and execute the "downward block".

## KARATE-DO APPLICATION

(1) Your opponent is in a ready position; you face him with your hands at your hip.
(2 & 3) As your opponent kicks at you, drop into a kneeling stance and block.

*In a fight, why would anyone stand with his hands on his hips? Is he so good he must even the odds? And, if the opponent is kicking, why drop down to block the kick? If the kick is so low that it cannot be reached to block with the hands, wouldn't a leg block be more effective?*

*Gichin Funakoshi renamed this kata Empi, meaning "flying swallow". However, the name Empi is a homophone of the word "empi" meaning elbow. This provides a useful clue in interpreting the kata. This form can be understood as containing techniques aimed at the pressure points in the empi region (from mid-forearm to mid-upper arm).*

# RYUKYU KEMPO APPLICATION

## PRESSURE POINTS: DIAGRAM 52A & 52B

(1) A larger opponent grabs your left wrist with his right hand.

(2 & 3) Roll your left hand around to turn his hand over and grasp his wrist on the pressure points L-7 and SI-6. Use your right hand to assist this movement as necessary.

(4) Twist strongly and draw his hand close to your body.

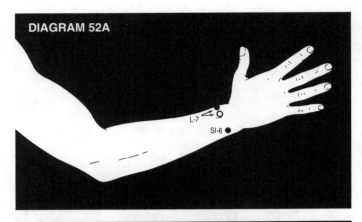

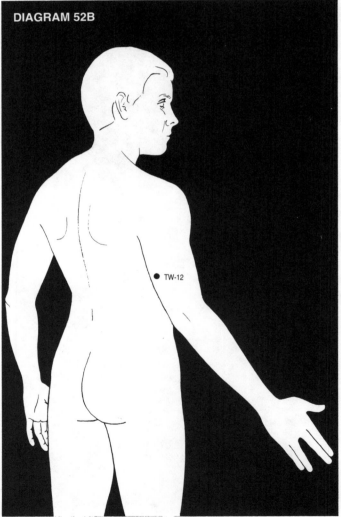

continued

## RYUKYU KEMPO APPLICATION
*Continued from previous page*

(5, 6 & 7) Strike down against TW-12, at the mid-point of the triceps with your right hand. (8, 9 & 10) Because your opponent is much larger, drop into a kneeling stance to add more weight to the strike, and break his arm, or drive him face-first into the floor.

**Note:** *A left-handed person will drop to the left knee as a right-handed person will feel more natural on the right knee.*

5

8

## KUSHANKU KATA

Kushanku is a very important kata in Okinawan history. Analysis of the kata indicates that Itosu may have been influenced by Kushanku when developing the five Pinan forms. For this reason, the following sequence can be found in Pinan 1 (though in some styles it appears with a sidekick as in the technique from Wansu described above). The particular movement described here is found in the version of Kushanku practiced among the shorin-ryu and isshin-ryu systems. Kushanku is also known as Kosokun or Kanku.

(1) Turning to the left, assume a left cat stance and draw both fists to the right hip, left fist on top. (2) Front kick with the left leg while striking with the left hand (some styles use a punch, others a hammer fist and others a backfist).

## KARATE-DO APPLICATION

(1) As your opponent prepares to attack from the left, face him in a left cat stance, with your hands at your right hip.
(2) As he charges with a right lunge punch, block the punch with your left fist as you kick with your left foot.

*The basic principle of stopping an attacker's rush with a defensive lead-leg kick is sound, and useful in free-fighting.· However, the stacking of the hands prior to the technique makes no sense at all.*

# RYUKYU KEMPO APPLICATION

### PRESSURE POINTS: DIAGRAM 53A & 53B

(1) Your opponent grabs your lapel with his right hand and threatens you with his left.

(2) Reach over his arm with your right hand, grasping his wrist firmly and pressing on H-6 and L-8. Reinforce this with your left hand.

(3) Twist his hand from your lapel.

(4) Pull his right arm forcefully to your right hip.

(5 & 6) Kick the inside of your attacker's left leg. At the same time, strike with your left hand to the side of his head, hitting either S-5 under the jaw with a hammer fist, or punching TW-17 under the ear.

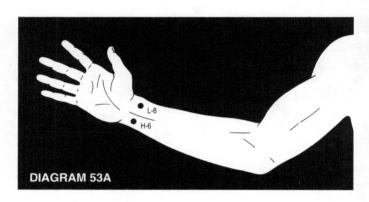

DIAGRAM 53A

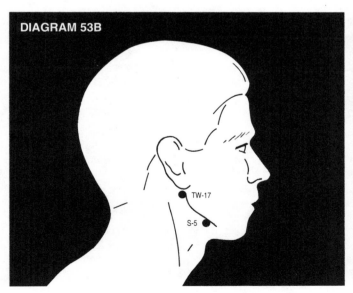

DIAGRAM 53B

## SEISAN KATA

Seisan kata (sometimes called Hangetsu) is found in many styles of karate. There are, in fact three distinct "families" of Seisan kata, which are quite different from one another. These are, the tomari/shuri-family (including isshin-ryu and shotokan), the Higaonna-family (including shito-ryu and goju-ryu) and the Uechi-family (pangainoon, or uechi-ryu). The sequence being demonstrated here is the only portion which can be clearly identified in all three families (even so, there are variances in exact performance).

(1) Begin in a right front stance, with the right hand held down and towards the left side of the body, and the left hand up and towards the right side. This is the "set" position.

(2 & 3) Sweep the right hand, palm up, to the right, performing a "ridge-hand block", while sweeping the left hand down and to the side in a "low open-hand block".

(4) Turn the right hand over and reach forward.

(5) Draw the right hand back as though grabbing and pulling.

## KARATE-DO APPLICATION

(1) You are fighting two opponents, one in front and one to your left.

(2) The opponent to the front attacks with a right punch, which you block with your right "ridge-hand block".  At the same time, the second attacker executes a right front kick.  This technique you block with your left hand, without looking away from the opponent in front.

continued

## KARATE-DO APPLICATION

*Continued from previous page*

(3) Turn your right hand over and grasp the arm of the attacker in front.

(4) Pull down on his arm.

*Obviously, this application is purely "stylized". The attacker on the left never follows up on his front kick. The attacker in front leaves his arm out to be grabbed and pulled. And, at no time does the defender counter-attack. In recognition of this, some schools teach that there is a chop to the neck concealed in the action of turning the right hand over and reaching out. However, even with this addition, the left hand — and the kicker it supposedly blocks — is ignored.*

## RYUKYU KEMPO APPLICATION

### PRESSURE POINTS: DIAGRAM 54A & 54B

(1) Your only opponent prepares to punch you with his right hand.

(2 & 3) As he punches, you deflect the attack with your right hand then grasp his wrist on the pressure points H-6 & L-8 with your left hand.

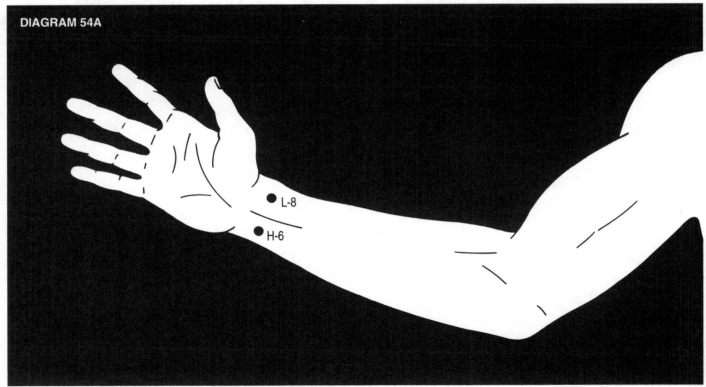

DIAGRAM 54A

L-8

H-6

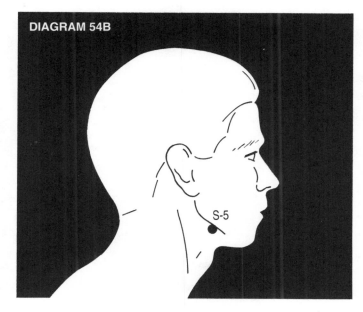

DIAGRAM 54B

S-5

continued

## RYUKYU KEMPO APPLICATION

*Continued from previous page*

(4 & 5) Pulling his captured hand down and to the left, you simultaneously strike with a right ridge-hand under the jaw at S-5.

(6 & 7) Reach around behind the attacker's head and grab his hair or ear (in ancient times, his top-knot) with your right hand and pull forcefully to wrench his neck.

**Note**: *A "ridgehand strike" is one of the most effective techniques for releasing your energy into your opponent.*

## SEIUCHIN KATA

Seiuchin originated in China and is characteristic of the Naha styles. But, this kata has come to be widely practiced among diverse systems, including certain schools of shorin-ryu.

(1) Bring your right fist across your body in the same manner as the set position for a "side block", and place your left palm against it.
(2) Step with your right foot to the diagonal and perform a "reinforced block", your right hand moving as in a "side block" with your left hand pressing against it.
(3) Step forward along the diagonal with your left leg into a side horse stance and perform a left "downward block".

## KARATE-DO APPLICATION

(1) An opponent prepares to attack you from the right diagonal.

(2)  As he steps in with a right punch, block his attack with a right reinforced block.

(3) As he continues his attack by kicking, step into a horse stance and block with your left hand.

*This application can be criticized at several points, such as using the small bone of the arm to block kicks, or stepping into an oncoming attack.  But the real problem is summed up in this saying: "If you need two hands to block the punch, you're in the wrong fight."*

# RYUKYU KEMPO APPLICATION

## PRESSURE POINTS: DIAGRAM 55A & 55B

(1) Your opponent grabs your right wrist with his right hand.

(2) Press your left hand over his right hand to trap, and circle your hands towards your left side.

(3) Bring your hands up and to the right (as in a "side block") as you angle yourself on the diagonal to your attacker.

1

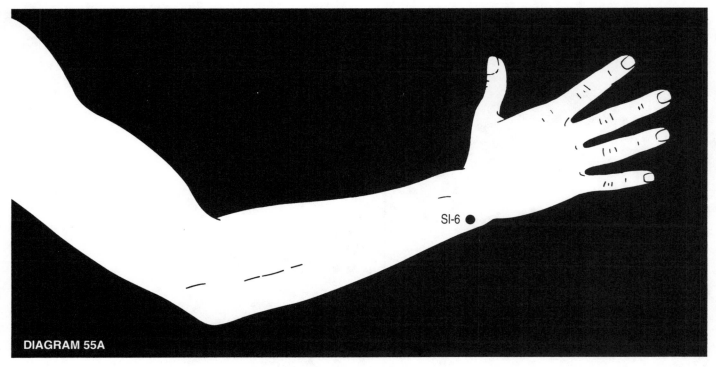

SI-6

**DIAGRAM 55A**

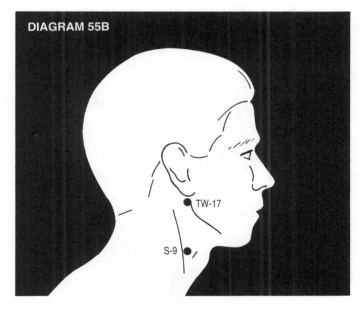

DIAGRAM 55B

TW-17

S-9

223

continued

# RYUKYU KEMPO APPLICATION

*Continued from previous page*

(4) Press the knuckle of your right fist down onto your attacker's wrist point SI-6.

(5) Push down, dropping him to the floor.

(6, 7 & 8) Grab his right hand with your right hand and pull towards your right hip as you step in and strike the side of the attacker's neck at S-9 or under the ear at TW-17 with your left fist.

## SANCHIN KATA

Sanchin is one of the most basic and common forms practiced. Like most kata, there are several versions which differ slightly (for example, some perform the movement given here with open hands). Primarily, the kata is done as a breathing exercise, and little attention is given to its interpretation. Nonetheless, this kata contains effective pressure point techniques.

(1) Step forward with the left leg into a front stance (many styles turn the toes inward and tense the leg muscles to form sanchin-dachi) and cross the arms in front of your chest.
(2) Bring your hands forward and apart.
(3) Draw your hands back slightly, about even with the edges of your body.

## KARATE-DO APPLICATION

(1) Your opponent grabs you by the lapels with both hands.

(2) Bring your arms up inside his, and force his arms loose by pressing outward with the edges of your wrists.

*While this application looks good on paper, it cannot work. As pointed out before, the action of pressing the arms outward (abduction) is much weaker than the action of drawing the arms inward (adduction).*

*(3) By bringing your arms up inside his, you are giving him the mechanical advantage. All the attacker has to do is squeeze his arms together and you are trapped. This karate-do application is an example of the saying, "Now I've got you right where you want me."*

# RYUKYU KEMPO APPLICATION

## PRESSURE POINTS: DIAGRAM 56A & 56B

(1) As your opponent grabs you by the lapels with both hands, bring your arms up outside his arms.

(2) Strike in and back against the point LI-10 on the outside of his forearm near the elbow. This corresponds to the "set" position in the kata movement.

1

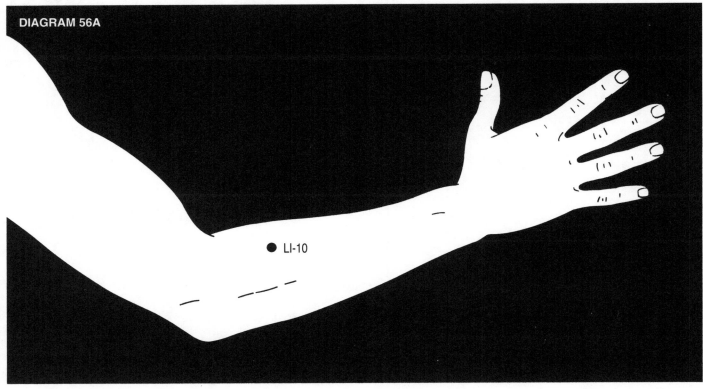

DIAGRAM 56A

● LI-10

2

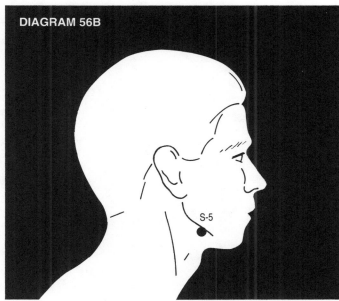

DIAGRAM 56B

S-5

continued

## RYUKYU KEMPO APPLICATION

*Continued from previous page*

(3) As a result of the strike to the arms points, your opponent's head will come forward, exposing his jaw.

(4, 5 & 6) Strike upwards with both fists hitting the groove of the jaw at S-5 on both sides of the head to knock your opponent unconscious.

**Caution: This technique strikes to both sides of the head, so it should never actually be performed, but only indicated during practice.**

## BASSAI KATA

The kata Bassai (or Patsai) is well known in karate, and even practiced among some Korean styles. While there are several different versions, the opening movement is essentially the same in all the variants.

(1) Begin with your feet together and your right fist in your left palm at head height.
(2 & 3) Draw your hands downward to groin level as you assume a left cat stance.

continued

## BASSAI KATA

*Continued from previous page*

(4 & 5) Jump forward with the right leg while drawing the hands to the left side.
(6) And draw the left leg up immediately to assume a cross-legged stance.  At the same time, perform a "reinforced block", your right hand moving as in a "side block" with your left open hand pressed against it.

4

## KARATE-DO APPLICATION

(1) Threatened by an assailant, you assume a left cat stance with your hands held low.
(2) As your opponent attacks with a right punch, leap directly towards him.
(3 & 4) And block his attack with your right arm, reinforced by your left.

*"Leap directly into an attack" is not exactly good advice. Yet, that is what the karate-do interpretation implies. Karate instructors will sometimes talk of "sen no sen" or "superior initiative", that mythical quality of killer ferocity, freight train fighting, and kamikaze spirit which supposedly makes a champion.*

*Certainly it has its place; but "sen no sen" is not about charging in recklessly. It is about an attitude of the heart, reflected in boundless determination, regardless of the tactics used to express that determination. However, discussions of "sen no sen" are essentially smoke screens to conceal the fact that karate instructors frequently haven't a clue as to the meaning of the opening movement of Bassai.*

# RYUKYU KEMPO APPLICATION

(1) An attacker verbally threatens while poking at your chest with his right hand.

(2, 3 & 4) Catch his hand with your left hand, and grasp his index finger with your right.

continued

## RYUKYU KEMPO APPLICATION
*Continued from previous page*

(5 & 6) As you assume a left cat stance, bend his index finger back and press it down, locking it against your left thigh.

(7) Suddenly, twist your opponent's captured finger up and to your left.

(8 & 9) Jump past the outside of his right leg, holding his finger firmly.

continued

## RYUKYU KEMPO APPLICATION

*Continued from previous page*

(10 ,11 ,12 ,13 & 14) Drop into a cross-legged stance, applying the full weight of your body against his captured finger to drive him to the ground.

**Note:** *The structure of the cross-legged stance prevents you from falling on your opponent.*

## SHISOCHIN KATA

In our demonstrations we have shown how karate-do applications often have no relation whatsoever to the actual application of a technique. However, it is not always the case that the common application is hopelessly off-base. Sometimes the application is essentially correct, but a lack of pressure point knowledge makes the technique unreliable. Simply by using the pressure points, the technique can become virtually 100%. To illustrate this, we will give an example from the goju-ryu kata shisochin.

(1) Begin in a right front stance with your right hand up and your left hand down.
(2) Bring your left hand up near your chest.
(3) Pivot on the balls of your feet, turning to the left and changing to a left front stance. At the same time, press with your right arm.

## KARATE-DO APPLICATION

(1) Your opponent prepares to attack you with a left punch.
(2) As he punches, catch his arm with your left hand.
(3) Strike his elbow with your right arm in an effort to break it.

*This application is essentially correct, except that it is virtually impossible to strike someone's elbow and break it. Perhaps, if your timing was perfect, and you were able to catch his arm and pull it sharply so as to over-extend it, it might be possible to seriously injure the elbow. However, in a fight that is a lot of if's.*

# RYUKYU KEMPO APPLICATION

## PRESSURE POINTS: DIAGRAM 57A & 57B

(1 & 2) As your opponent attacks with a left punch, catch his wrist with your left hand, grabbing pressure points H-6 and L-8.

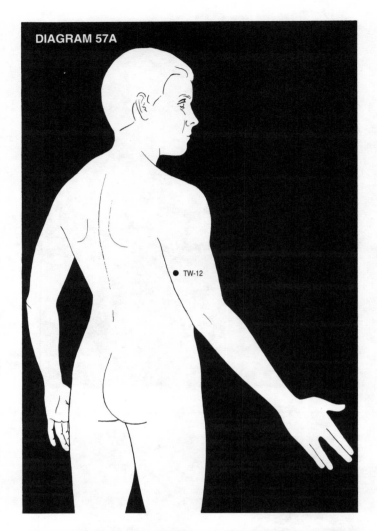

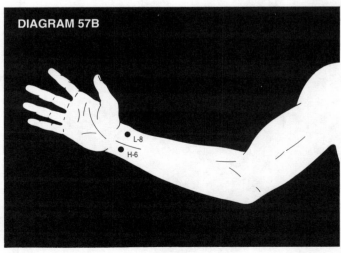

249

continued

## RYUKYU KEMPO APPLICATION
*Continued from previous page*

(3)  With your right arm, strike him mid-triceps on TW-12.

(4 & 5) Use the body turning to drive him to the ground.

# APPENDIX A:
# Grabbing the Wrist Points

Catching and grabbing the pressure points on the wrist is one of the most fundamental skills in kyusho-jitsu, so some attention must be given to the details of this action.

When grabbing the wrist from the outside, the pressure points H-6 and L-8 (diagram 59) are used. The fingertips and the joint of the thumb can be used to press on the points. Dig the fingers into the wrist, squeezing the points against the underlying bone, and towards the hand (photo 1 & 2).

When grabbing the wrist from the inside, points L-7 and SI-6 are used (diagram 60) Squeeze SI-6 against the ulnar bone and towards the hand with the joint of the thumb or the finger-tips. Point L-7 must be torqued for maximum effect.

When grabbing from above, squeeze with the fingers on SI-6 and roll the thumb across L-7 as if to physically move the point to the outside of the arm. Then squeeze the thumb firmly against the radial bone (photo 3 & 4).

When grabbing from below, squeeze with the thumb on SI-6 and roll the fingers across L-7 towards the outside of the arm. Then squeeze the fingers firmly against the radial bone (photo 5 & 6).

**Left:** George A. Dillman uses "small circle" theory of Prof. Wally Jay to drop Ian Waite of New Zealand during a photo shoot for Rainbow Publications.
Photo by Doug Churchill

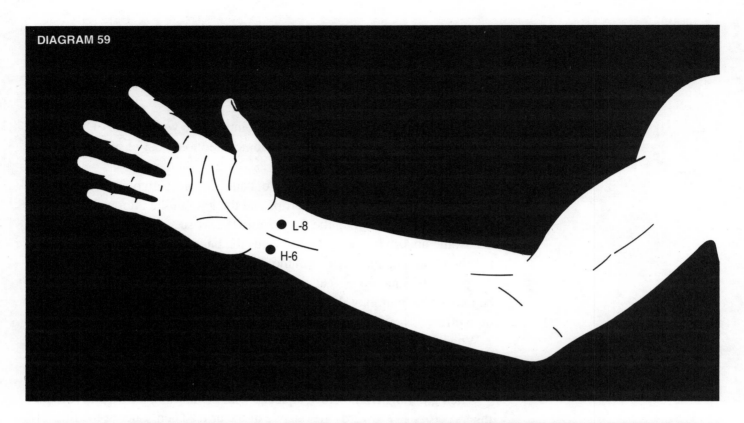

DIAGRAM 59

L-8

H-6

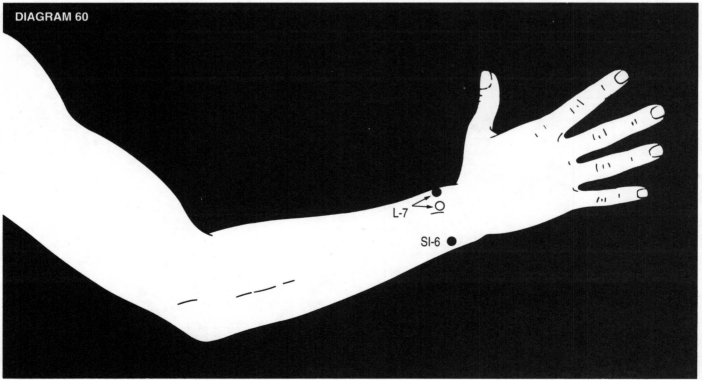

DIAGRAM 60

L-7

SI-6

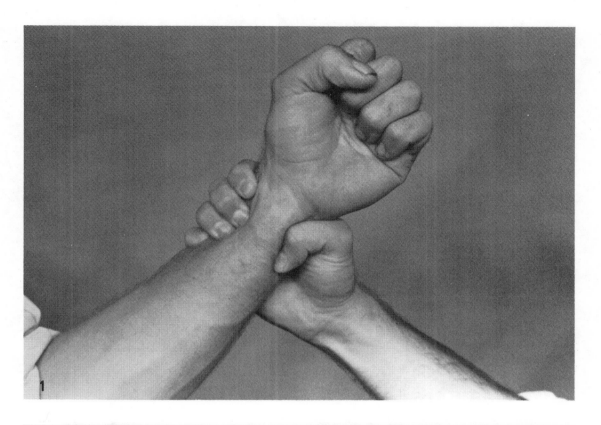

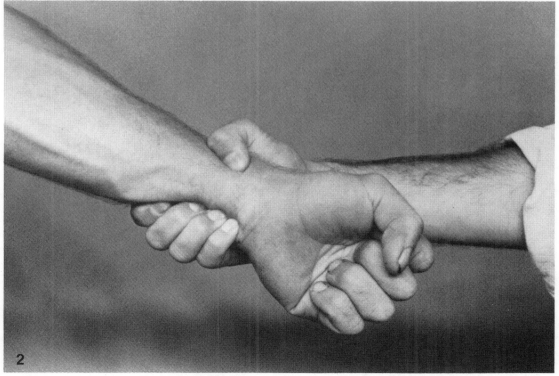

continued

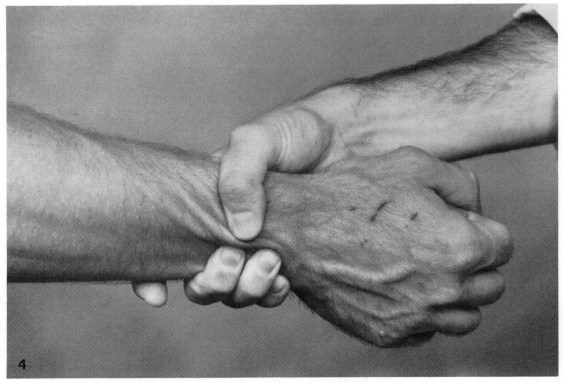

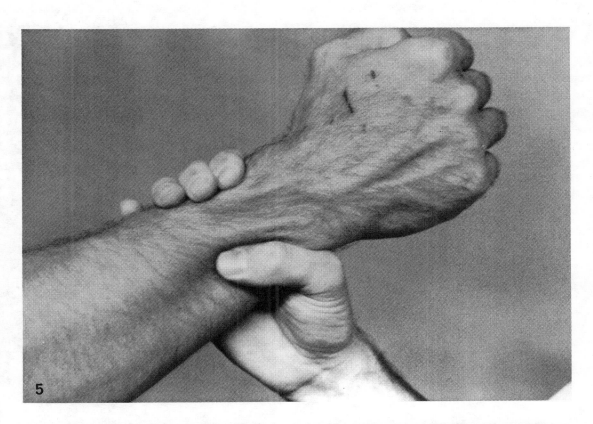

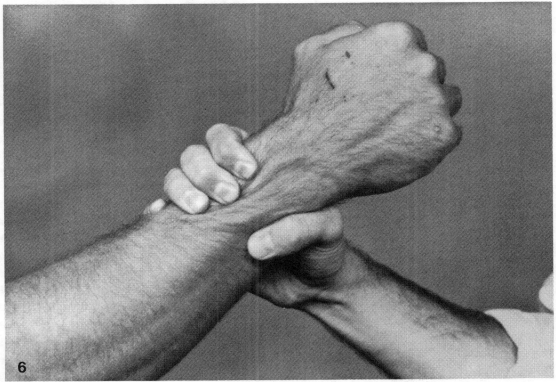

# APPENDIX B:
# How to Catch a Punch

Though arm pressure points can be activated simply by hitting or touching them, most Ryukyu kempo responses against a punch prefer to catch the arm and grab directly on the points for greater control. In fact, a general rule of thumb in interpreting kata is that the hiki-te, or "withdrawing hand" (the hand that comes back to your hip) is always grabbing and pulling your opponent. If the hiki-te is closed into a fist, the grab is on the wrist (or finger) pressure points (photo 1). If the hiki-te is open, the grab is higher up, on points near the elbow (photo 2).

Catching a punch is a specialized skill that does require training and practice. A few exceptional martial artists can simply catch a wrist, like snatching an insect out of the air. However, most individuals must use a specific technique which relies on the principle of muchimi, or "adhesion" to acquire the grab.

The following are the two major methods for catching a punch. You will note that these methods follow certain important principles:

1. Always block using two bones and the muscle portion of the outside of the forearm. The bones of the arm (in particular the ulna) are easily broken. Blocking with only one bone exposes your own arm to risk of injury.

2. The longer your arm is in contact with your opponent's arm, the easier it is to grab. Prolonged contact allows you to sense the location of his pressure points, and to grab without looking.

3. Use "adhesion" (muchimi) to control the movement of your opponent's arm. Once a punch has failed, your opponent will try to withdraw his arm. By sticking to the opponent's arm you slow down the recoil and give yourself more time to grab.

**Left:** Carl Daigrepont of Kenner, LA uses pressure points and the Dillman Theory to stop an arm-grab attempt.

1

2

## TWO HANDED CATCH

(1 & 2) As your opponent punches with his right fist, slap his fist towards your right ear with your left hand. This deflects his punch, but also makes it difficult for him to recoil.

(3) Bring your right arm up, rubbing the back of your right forearm (with muchimi) against his arm. Once this contact is made, you know immediately where his arm is.

(4) Pull your right arm down and grab his pressure points.

Practice this movement until it is a single rapid and continuous motion. Practice grabbing at the wrist points, the mid-forearm points and the elbow area points.

(A) This action may be performed from the outside (as in the example) or from the inside. The outside is preferable because it moves you away from a possible follow-up punch delivered with his free arm.

## ONE HANDED CATCH

(1) As your opponent punches, reach out with your right arm to make contact with the arm at the beginning of his motion.

(2) Move with his punch, drawing your arm back and sticking to his arm. This slight adhesion will slow down his recoil.

(3 & 4) Pull your arm down, and grab his pressure points. Make sure to jerk as you grab to keep him off balance.

continued

## ONE HANDED CATCH
*Continued from previous page*

A one-handed grab is very difficult because it depends on making contact with his arm early in the punching motion. This means that you must be able to anticipate his action. However, it also allows you to move into his attack (irimi-waza, "entering technique") to monopolize his space and instantly counter as the following example demonstrates:

(5 & 6) As your opponent attacks with a right punch, step forward with your left leg outside his attack and catch his arm using a one-handed catch.

(7) In one continuing motion, pull him forward drawing your right hand to your hip, and strike him on the body, with your left fist.

**Note:** *This is an application of the action of stepping forward into a side stance and performing a "downward block" which is found in many kata.*

5

# APPENDIX C:
# Altered States of Consciousness

When we hear the words "knocked out" we are expecting someone lying limp on the floor. However, the term "knock-out" is much broader than that. Even in boxing there is a recognized "technical" knock-out, when one fighter has not fallen over, yet is clearly unable to defend himself.

From a strategic standpoint, many Ryukyu kempo techniques require that an opponent be rendered "unconscious" but remain standing. An example of this is the technique from the kata Seisan which we have described. In that application the defender requires time to grasp the attacker's hair, an act which would be impossible if the opponent was struggling and fighting. If, however, the attacker is falling to the ground, the neck-wrench can not be applied.

For this reason there are three levels of "knock-outs" performed.

1. Complete unconsciousness and cessation of body function. In other words, a four pressure point knock-out, or a hard three point knock-out. Your opponent is on the floor with no awareness at all.

2. Complete loss of motor control. This means that your opponent has been knocked to the floor and cannot regain immediate control of his or her arms and legs. Yet, he or she may be conscious in the sense that there is some awareness of what is happening. This is generally a three point knock-out.

3. Impairment of motor control and altered perceptions. This is a "standing knock-out". In this state your opponent is still standing, but is temporarily unable to think clearly or move intentionally. This is a "2 1/2" point (in other words, a light three point) knock out, and is used to render the opponent helpless while the defense continues with a more serious finishing technique (such as the neck-wrench).

Generally, in seminars and demonstrations it is the "standing knock-outs" which are performed. And, if you examine the applications we have presented, you will find that many of them depend on this type of knock-out somewhere in the middle of the technique.

**Left:** Jim Corn (left) uses wrist point and shows the effect when opposite head points are just tapped.

# SELECTED BIBLIOGRAPHY & SOURCES

BISHOP, Mark
**Okinawan Karate—Teachers, Styles and Secret Techniques**
A & C Black LTD
London, 1989

EGAMI, Shigeru
**The Heart of Karate-Do**
Kodansha International
Tokyo, 1980

DILLMAN, George A.
**Pressure Point Video Instructional Series**
Dillman Karate International
Reading, PA

FUNAKOSHI, Gichin
**Ryukyu Kempo: Karate 1922**

**Karate-Do Kyohan**
tr. T. Ohshima
Kodansha International
Tokyo, 1973

**Karate-Do Nyumon**
Kodansha International
Tokyo, 1988

HISATAKA, Masayuki
**Scientific Karate-Do**
Japan Publications
Tokyo, 1976

JAY, Wally
**Small-Circle Jujitsu**
Ohara Publications
Burbank, CA 1989

MOTOBU, Choki
**Okinawa Kempo Karate-Jutsu**
tr. Seiyu Oyata
Ryukyu Imports
Olathe, KS 1977

NAGAMINE, Shoshin
**The Essence of Okinawan Karate-do**
Charles E. Tuttle
Rutland, Vermont 1976

OHASHI, Wataru
**Do-It-Yourself Shiatsu**
E.P. Dutton
New York, 1976

SHANGHAI COLLEGE OF
TRADITIONAL MEDICINE
**Acupuncture a Comprehensive Text**
tr. John O'Connor & Dan Bensky
Eastland Press
Seattle, 1981

SHUM, Leung
**Eagle Claw Kung Fu**
Leung Shum
New York, 1980

THOMAS, Chris
*"Will Dillman's Tactics Work on the Streets?"*
Inside Kung Fu, Oct. '89

*"Karate's Conspiracy of Silence: Do Deadly Pressure Point Strikes Really Exist in Karate Kata?"*
Black Belt, Jan. '90

*"George Dillman Fights Back! Controversial Karateka Answers His Critics"*
Black Belt, Apr. '91

*"Kata in Ryukyu Kempo"*
Karate Kung-Fu Illustrated, Oct. '91

UESHIBA, Morihei
**Budo: Teachings of the Founder of Aikido**
Kodansha International
Tokyo, 1991

WONG, Douglas
**Kung-Fu: the Way of Life**
Unique Publications
Hollywood, 1979

YANG, Jwing-Ming
**Analysis of Shaolin Chin Na**
Yang's Martial Arts Assoc.
Jamaica Plain, Mass 1987

**Left:** George and Kimberly Dillman complete their fifth tour teaching packed house seminars in New Zealand and Australia in 1991. Here Kim demonstrates a self-defense technique on George as he grabs her from behind.

Graphic design by:

Sergio Onaga